TAILGATE PARTIES

TAILGATE PARTIES

24 menus for gourmet picnics and outdoor entertaining

by Susan Wyler

A Particular Palate Cookbook™
Harmony Books/New York

A Particular Palate Cookbook

Copyright © 1984 by Susan Wyler

Published by Harmony Books, a division of Crown Publishers, Inc.,
One Park Avenue, New York, New York 10016, and simultaneously
in Canada by General Publishing Company Limited

HARMONY, PARTICULAR PALATE, and colophons are
trademarks of Crown Publishers, Inc.

Manufactured in the United States of America

Library of Congress Cataloging in Publication Data

Wyler, Susan
　　Tailgate parties.

　　1. Outdoor cookery　2. Picnicking.　3. Menus
I. Title.
TX823.W94 1984　　641.5'78　　　84-3795
ISBN 0-517-55441-0 (pbk.)

10 9 8 7 6 5 4 3 2 1

First Edition

Contents

Acknowledgments

Thanks to Virginia Barber, who made this book possible for me; my excellent editor Harriet Bell, who knew what she wanted and helped shape this book; and all my other friends, especially Russell, who helped shop and eat.

Introduction

Dining outdoors has always had an aura of romance attached to it. The fresh smell of the open air, the graceful light of a sunny blue sky and the excitement of a day's activity add to the natural pleasures of sharing a meal with good friends. Outdoor entertaining has come into its own in recent years. With the growing interest in food preparation and presentation, even picnicking has become more elegant.

That's where the tailgate party comes in. What differentiates a tailgate from an ordinary picnic is that it is more of an event. Named for the back end of the station wagon that was traditionally used as both larder and buffet table at football games, the tailgate implies a vehicle for transportation and useful service. No knapsack full of minimal rations here, no soggy sandwiches and run-of-the-mill candy bars. The trunk can hold everything you want to bring along, including food, beverages, coolers, portable grills, picnic baskets and all the accoutrements, from paper plates to fine bone china. Unrestricted by weight and volume, the spread can become as elaborate as you choose to make it; service is both easier and as much of a production as you wish. It is not uncommon for ardent tailgaters to turn a parking lot or picnic ground into a formal dining room replete with china, silver, tablecloth and even candelabra.

Because tailgates are linked to occasions that occur at different times of the year, the foods tend to be seasonal. Fresh ripe tomatoes, sweet corn and blueberries, perfect for the Fourth of July, give way to heartier foods like pork, cheese and apples in the fall. In summer, iced soups and chilled salads, barbecued meats and fish whet appetites dulled by the heat, while the chill of winter dictates spicy stews and mugs of steaming, hot soup to thaw frosty fingers numbed in the bleachers on a blustery November day.

No matter what the time of year, tailgate parties are festive, and the food should contribute to the high spirits. This book is organized into menus to make it easy for you to prepare a complete feast. Each is made up of at least two recipes for you to prepare and additional foods that can be purchased. Each of the menus is designed with a certain season in mind. Some are exceptionally quick and easy. Others require a barbecue grill. A few are especially luxurious and some are suited for an unusually large crowd. Many of the menus have themes with an international flair: a Mexican fiesta for the Superbowl, a Spanish picnic for a country outing, all-American fare for the Fourth of July.

A good friend of mine who graduated from the University of Illinois told me how popular tailgates are there. At their annual homecoming football game, they take their partying so seriously that a prize is offered for the best tailgate. One year, he remembered, the winners constructed an authentic Hawaiian luau—complete with sand and palm trees!

You may not feel like going quite that far, but a little extra attention to theme, atmosphere and the appropriate accessories can add greatly to the festivity of a tailgate. Set a Mexican table with a bright-colored serape and cactus; use a plaid blanket and basket of pine cones for a fall leaves party; pull out your best china and silver for A Day at the Races feast.

Because it is indeed a movable feast, tailgate dining does pose some challenges. When planning the menu, both the cook and outdoor conditions must be taken into account. The picnic is in fact a dinner party, but the cook has no stove, except perhaps a small charcoal grill. Refrigeration is reduced to the square-inch capacity of an ice chest or thermal cooler. The party often shoves off early in the day, leaving little time for preparation on the day of the event. And finally, when you do sit down and eat, whether on the ground or in the stands, a tailgate is, in the end, a picnic, with all the juggling of plates and cups and the cheerful informality that the term implies.

All these conditions pose design problems that this book has tried to overcome. Much of the food can be prepared at least a day in advance. Many of the recipes are simple and easy. An attempt has been made to create food that keeps well, and many of the dishes are designed to taste best at room temperature. The foods must be attractive in themselves, requiring no fussy garnishes. And the service must be simple: meats cut into bite-size pieces where possible, soup poured into mugs, finger food where appropriate.

All told, it's great food for entertaining— outdoors or in. Many tailgate events are celebrated in a number of ways. A lucky few have tickets to the Superbowl game. Most fans have to be content in front of the television set, but the same spirit and the same call for merriment, food and drink abound. Most of the recipes in this book can be doubled or halved easily, tailored to the kinds of parties you like to throw.

Dishes that work well on a picnic table will do brilliantly on a buffet. Advance preparations geared for an outing can only make life easier for the at-home hostess who needs some time to relax before guests arrive and cannot possibly prepare all the food at the last moment. I'm a great believer in the maxim that to create a successful dinner party the cook must become a guest in her own home. If you are relaxed and enjoying yourself, your party is sure to be a hit.

Of all the ingredients necessary to a successful tailgate party, organization is the key factor. The principles involved in planning an elaborate picnic are the same as for any entertaining you do, but with the following differences:

You will be serving under somewhat primitive circumstances, with limited refrigeration and a small heat source, if any.

Most of the food must be prepared ahead of time and transported to another place.

You cannot forget anything because you will not be in a position to run into the kitchen for an extra plate or to phone your local market to send over an extra case of soda.

Make a list to help you keep track of the details. The extra effort you make in planning ahead will pay off in the end.

Begin by planning the menu. To help you, I've grouped the recipes into 24 complete menus, designed for a variety of occasions. Each has an accompanying list of special equipment you will need for transporting and serving the food. The menus range from quick and easy spreads featuring a couple of simply prepared recipes, like the Country Outing on page 71, to elegant, sophisticated meals, like A Day at the Races on page 44, tailored to special occasions when you feel like expending the extra effort. I've tried to balance flavors and, being fond of a variety of foods myself, offer an assortment of recipes from a number of international cuisines. (The asterisks in each menu refer to the recipes included in each tailgate party.)

Despite the intended assets of these menus, please remember: They are just suggestions. Feel free to pick and choose, to mix and match recipes from different menus. Do only as much as you feel like. Split the cooking of a menu with a friend, or buy prepared foods to fill in. One of the most memorable picnics I ever went on was completely spur-of-the-moment. The food we threw together consisted of a chunk of pungent cheese, a spicy hard sausage, a jar of home-preserved olives, a loaf of crusty Italian bread, a bottle of chilled wine and a bunch of black grapes. A tailgate party almost by definition is usually a more elaborate affair, the prepared food and service being part of the festivities, but always remember how much fun you can have with the bare basics and build from there.

Once you've planned your menu, the next step is to make a shopping list. Include the ingredients needed to make the recipes you've chosen, plus any other items you may want to bring along: bread, cheese, fruit, beverages, paper plates, charcoal if appropriate.

Set up a rough timetable of preparation for yourself. I have indicated which recipes can be done a week or more ahead and can be frozen or held in the refrigerator. Most of the cooking can be staggered over a one- or two-day period before the party. Try to plan for as little last-minute preparation and assembly as possible. The recipes and menu introductions include information on do-ahead preparation and tips on packing the food.

Before starting out, consult the checklist on page 15. Be sure to include all the dishes you prepared as well as any other items on your menu. It's next to impossible to keep everything in your head, and you'll find this list a valuable planning tool.

Invariably, something gets left behind. If and when that happens to you, my advice is to ignore it if possible, or if it's an obvious or inconvenient omission, turn it into a laugh and make the best of the situation. Some of my best parties have included a "blooper," like a filling that didn't set and by necessity became a sauce, or caramel that softened and stuck everyone's teeth together, inspiring a spate of after-dinner dental jokes. There's something about a touch of imperfection, in an otherwise delicious meal, that tends to make everyone feel human and a little more relaxed.

BEVERAGES Everyone gets thirsty, especially during a day's activities in the open air and after eating a lot of tasty food. It seems as if beverages are always the first things that run out at outdoor parties. Don't underestimate how much you will need.

Beer, wine and liquor. Consider the occasion, the length of time the party will last, the type of food being served and the amount of driving to be done at the end of the event. I've given suggestions with each menu, but feel free to mix and match your own.

Coffee and tea. Hot or iced, depending on the season of the year, are always welcome after every meal. Allow two cups per person and don't forget the cream and sugar!

Soda and juice. Large quantities of beverages for quenching thirst are best bought in cans and plastic bottles and transported in a cooler filled with ice. I save old plastic soda bottles, rinse them out and fill them with water or juice using a small-necked funnel.

CLEANING UP It's not the best part of the party, but bringing home the dirty dishes has to be dealt with. At least you have the satisfaction of knowing the pots and pans are already done. The great joy of paper plates and plastic cups, forks and knives is that they can simply be thrown away. Unless you are in the middle of the wilderness, every picnic area has trash receptacles.

If you've opted for durable plastic or china, however, the remains have to be carted back. Even if you've eaten from paper, there are still carrying containers and serving dishes to account for.

My solution is large, heavy-duty plastic trash bags. If there is running water or a stream, I rinse everything quickly and just toss it in the bag. Breakable plates should be rinsed if possible, stacked neatly, wrapped in the plastic bag and then packed in a sturdy picnic basket or other protective container.

The only really problematic item to bring home can be the grill, which gets very hot and very dirty. Be sure to cook long enough before heading home to allow the grill time to cool off. Dump out the warm coals and fill the hot grill with any remaining ice or water left in your cooler. Give the grill a few moments to cool, then pour out the water. A cool grill can be stuffed inside another large plastic bag and taken home in the trunk.

Equipment

Transporting foods for a tailgate party and keeping them fresh throughout the day requires a bit of ingenuity and some special equipment. If you plan on tailgating regularly, it is worth investing in at least a few of the basics. Look for them in gift boutiques, food equipment and cookware shops, better department stores and sporting goods and hardware stores. Mail-order cookware and gift catalogs are a particularly good source for tailgate equipment (see Source Guide, page 123). The following is a rather general description of some of the specialty picnic items I recommend to make your tailgate party a success.

PICNIC BASKETS You can carry your food in anything you want, but a traditional basket is both practical and attractive. They are not cheap, generally ranging from $75 on up, but the good ones contain everything you need for a grand alfresco dinner party, and they make marvelous gifts. Some contain padded bags for wine, cheeseboard and knife and decorative storage/serving containers as well. A few are packed with real china, but most of them, even the better baskets, opt for the unbreakable.

COOLER AND THERMOS Jet-age technology has given us wonderful products for keeping food hot and cold. It is handy to have a couple of thermos bottles for beverages and one large,

wide-mouthed container for soups and stews.

There are all sorts of carriers on the market for wine bottles, and if you are a serious wine buff, it pays to investigate the possibilities. The two main functions of these carriers are to prevent breakage and to keep the wine cool.

Coolers come in all shapes and sizes these days. They are fairly inexpensive, and, with the handy gel-packs that can be frozen ahead to keep food chilled for hours, spoilage at picnics is much less of a problem than it used to be. Nevertheless, always err on the side of caution. Ice chests are still handy for large quantities of soft drinks or beer and can double as extra storage space for well-wrapped foods that need extra preservation. The Brinsdon HC-10 is a combination cooler/warmer that plugs into the cigarette lighter of a car without stressing the battery for six hours. It provides double the amount of storage space because no ice is necessary.

COVERED CONTAINERS Tightly lidded containers are a must for tailgate transport. It is well worth investing in a large assortment of shapes and sizes. Convenient plastic food storage equipment, such as covered containers and bowls, come in every shape and size and are worth taking a look at.

DISHES, UTENSILS, GLASSWARE If your picnic basket is not preequipped, you have some decisions to make here. China is fun once in a blue moon, but it is more trouble than it's worth to transport. For permanent ware, sturdy plastic is a happy compromise. Williams-Sonoma offers a compact set of Italian plastic that includes two large serving bowls and six each dinner plates, dessert plates, bowls, cups, knives, forks and spoons and a serving fork and spoon—all for close to $40. Durable stackable plastic plates and colorful disposable lightweight plastic plates, both widely available, are good choices for picnicking.

Another alternative is paper—not all that unattractive these days. Lightweight and disposable, paper goods come in a nice array of colors and attractive patterns. If you do opt for paper, make sure it is coated to prevent moisture or grease from leaking through and to tolerate hot foods. Nothing is more unappetizing than having your plate dissolve in your lap.

As for utensils, sturdy plastic is all right, though I prefer metal. It is not hard to transport silverware, and the only care to be taken is to count the pieces as you clean up so no pieces get tossed in the trash.

I like to have a good supply of hot beverage cups because I frequently use them for soup on a picnic. Cups can also be used for wine, though some baskets come equipped with real glasses. There are some good-quality plastic wine goblets on the market that are reasonably good looking and worth looking into.

GRILLS Grills are very much a matter of personal taste and experience. You'll probably get the best results from what you are accustomed to using. Nonetheless, if you are shopping for a new grill or one suitable for tailgating, keep in mind that charcoal grills come in three basic designs: tray and rack, covered kettle and hibachi.

I am partial to the kettle grill, which lets you adjust the temperature of the coals through a system of air vents. The cover helps retain moisture in foods and allows for slower cooking, which is especially useful for larger cuts of meat. For quick, short-cooking barbecues, like kebabs and steaks, little hibachis work quite well. The main problem with a portable grill is usually size. If you're cooking for a crowd, you might ask a friend to bring along a second grill. You'll be surprised at how much food can be turned over on even a small rack if you keep practicing and get good at juggling.

One other specialty charcoal grill recently introduced is the indoor/outdoor Ichi (see Source Guide, page 123). Among its pluses are a sturdy, compact packing box that doubles as a carrying case, interchangeable griddle, grill rack and fitted skewer cooking surfaces, adaptability to plug-in electricity indoors or charcoal outdoors, and the Silverstone and ceramic coatings, which make cleaning a snap.

Tabletop portable propane gas grills are also widely available. These are quick and clean, but be sure to follow the manufacturers' instructions carefully.

A NOTE ON GRILLING

Whatever type of grill you use, remember that cooking directions can only be approximate. Heat will vary depending upon the design of the grill and type of fuel you use. In general, lump charcoal will heat up faster than briquets, but it is often difficult to start and burns out in little more than half an hour. Briquets tend to be easier to light, even though they take longer to get hot, and they will burn longer. In general, start the grill 30 to 45 minutes before you plan to cook. Your fire is ready for grilling when the coals are glowing red hot and are covered with a thin film of white ash.

To ensure good results whenever you are barbecuing, always keep an eye on the food!

EQUIPMENT CHECKLIST Before you leave the house, be sure you haven't left anything behind. Write out your menu, down to the bread and butter, and make sure each item has been packed. Here is a list that I find useful; it includes both staples and those little things that are always left behind.

Food	Salt and pepper
Beverages	Corkscrew
Plates	Cheeseboard and knife
Bowls	Serrated knife
Forks, knives, spoons	Charcoal for grill
Cups, mugs, glasses	Matches
Serving dishes	Ice pack for cooler
Serving utensils	Bottle opener
Tablecloth or picnic blanket	Garbage bags
Napkins	Car keys

TAILGATE FEASTS

Football Tailgate

As the word implies, the origin of tailgate parties has to do with station wagons. In all likelihood, the first tailgate took place at the back of a "woody." To my mind, the term suggests visions of burnished autumn leaves, plaid wool blankets, frosty puffs of breath collecting over steaming mugs of hot soup, and the occasion—football.

Whether the game to you means season tickets to the home professional team or a match pitting your alma mater against its arch rival, eating in any stadium poses the same challenges. This menu was designed for cold weather picnicking. Although it can be enjoyed before the game in the stadium parking lot it is largely finger food that you can nibble from your seats throughout the game. The feast consists of easy pick-up food—piquant chicken legs spiced with three mustards; broccoli florets and carrot sticks, steamed until crisp-tender, then marinated in a garlicky vinaigrette, and a superb cake. Be sure to bring along plenty of napkins. Serve the creamy hot tomato soup spiked with vodka in mugs as a first course or as a beverage to sip along with the other food. It is a guaranteed bench warmer and there is enough for seconds. For dessert, I've included a favorite recipe from my childhood, my grandmother's dark, moist Molasses-Raisin Cake. I love it with a glass of cold milk, but strong hot coffee is just as good and will counter the nippy weather.

This menu was designed to make it as easy on the cook as on the guests. All the food can be made a day ahead. Reheat the soup and add the vodka just before pouring it into the thermos. Serve the chicken at room temperature.

CREAMY TOMATO SOUP WITH VODKA

Serves 6–8

2 tablespoons unsalted butter
1 tablespoon olive oil
1 large leek (white and tender green), coarsely chopped
3 tablespoons all-purpose flour
1 can (13¾ ounces) chicken broth
1 can (35 ounces) Italian peeled tomatoes, with the liquid
¾ teaspoon basil
1 to 1½ teaspoons sugar (depending on the acidity of the tomatoes)
1½ teaspoons salt
¼ teaspoon freshly ground black pepper
Several dashes of cayenne pepper, or more to taste
½ cup heavy cream
¾ cup vodka

1. In a large nonaluminum saucepan or heatproof casserole, melt the butter in the oil over moderate heat. Add the leek and sauté, stirring occasionally, until softened but not browned, about 3 minutes. Add the flour and cook, stirring, for 2 minutes without coloring to make a roux.

2. Add the chicken broth, tomatoes and the liquid, basil, sugar, salt, black pepper, cayenne and 2 cups water. Bring to a boil, reduce heat, simmer uncovered, for 20 minutes.

3. Remove the soup from the heat and let it cool slightly. Purée in batches in a blender or food processor. Return the soup to the saucepan and reheat. Add the cream and simmer for 5 minutes. Before serving, stir in the vodka.

TRIPLE-MUSTARD DEVILED CHICKEN LEGS

Serves 4–6

3 pounds (about 12) chicken drumsticks
Salt and freshly ground black pepper
⅓ cup plus 2 tablespoons olive oil
1 teaspoon Tabasco sauce
2 tablespoons Dijon-style mustard
2 tablespoons Honeycup mustard
1 teaspoon dry mustard
1 teaspoon tarragon
1 teaspoon salt
½ teaspoon freshly ground black pepper
1 tablespoon minced shallot
2 teaspoons white wine vinegar
1½ cups fresh bread crumbs (made from 3 or
    4 slices firm-textured white bread)
½ cup sour cream

1. Season the drumsticks liberally with salt and pepper. Marinate in a mixture of ⅓ cup of olive oil and ¾ teaspoon of Tabasco at room temperature for 30 to 60 minutes, turning once or twice.

2. In a small bowl, combine the Dijon-style mustard, Honeycup mustard, dry mustard, tarragon, salt and pepper. Mix well. Stir in the shallot. Gradually blend in the vinegar, remaining 2 tablespoons olive oil and ¼ teaspoon Tabasco. Reserve 2 tablespoons of this mixture for the dipping sauce.

3. Set the broiler rack 6 to 8 inches from the heat and preheat the broiler. Remove the chicken from the marinade. Whisk the marinade into the remaining mustard mixture. Paint the drumsticks with this mixture. Place on the broiler pan and broil until browned, 4 to 5 minutes. Turn and broil until browned on the second side, 4 to 5 minutes longer.

4. Turn the legs again. Paint with the mustard mixture. Sprinkle with bread crumbs and pat them lightly so they adhere. Continue to broil for about 1 minute, or until the crumbs brown. Remove the pan from the broiler. Reduce oven temperature to 375°F.

5. Turn the legs and paint the exposed areas with the mustard mixture. Sprinkle with crumbs and pat to adhere. Bake the chicken until the crumbs are browned and the chicken is cooked through and no longer pink, 10 to 15 minutes. Serve hot, at room temperature or slightly chilled.

6. To make the dipping sauce, blend the reserved mustard mixture with the sour cream. Cover and refrigerate until serving time. If the dipping sauce thickens too much upon overnight refrigeration, thin out with a little milk, stirring it in 1 teaspoon at a time.

GRANDMA'S MOLASSES-RAISIN CAKE

I could never get the exact ingredients for this moist gingerbread from my grandmother, who measured in pinches and "little bits." Recently, in the back of a 1912 Caloric cookbook of hers, I discovered a cache of her recipes. One of them was her molasses cake, and here it is, as good as ever, spicy and not too sweet.

Serves 6–8

2 tablespoons unsalted butter
1 cup milk
1 tablespoon distilled white vinegar
2 cups all-purpose flour
1 teaspoon baking soda
1 teaspoon cinnamon
1 teaspoon ginger
⅛ teaspoon salt
1 egg
½ cup sugar
1 cup unsulphured molasses
1 cup raisins

1. Preheat the oven to 350°F. Butter a 9-inch-square baking pan. Melt the butter and let cool to tepid.

2. Stir together the milk and vinegar; set aside. This mixture will curdle and thicken.

3. Sift together the flour, baking soda, cinnamon, ginger and salt.

4. In a large bowl, whisk the egg and sugar until the mixture is pale and thick enough to ribbon, about 2 minutes. Beat in the melted butter.

5. Combine the molasses and the soured milk.

6. Alternately stir the dry and liquid ingredients into the egg mixture, about one-third at a time, until blended. Stir in the raisins.

7. Pour the batter into the buttered pan. Bake for 45 to 55 minutes, or until a tester comes out clean and the edges of the cake begin to pull away from sides of the pan.

Superbowl Party

MENU

Serves 6–8

Margaritas by the Batch*

Guacamole*

Tortilla Chips

Santa Fe Chili*

Bowls of Chopped Scallion or Onion, Grated Cheddar Cheese, Sour Cream, Chopped Black Olives

Orange-Radish Salad* (see page 42)

Mexican Hot Chocolate*

Sugar Cookies

Tangerines

SPECIAL EQUIPMENT

Thermos for margaritas, chili and hot chocolate

Sealed container for guacamole

Serving spoon for chili

Mugs for chili

Spoons for chili

Mugs for Mexican Hot Chocolate

Not everyone is lucky enough to have tickets to the most popular sporting event of the year. If you are one of the millions who are not, chances are you are gathered in front of the television set with a group of close friends on Super Sunday. Superbowl parties can be as much fun as the game itself. For such festive occasions, I like to serve food that guests can help themselves to during commercials or the half-time show.

Whether it is the tequila in the margaritas or the glowing warmth engendered by the spiciness of the food, good cheer and high spirits always seem to go hand in hand with Mexican food with an American accent. Tex-Mex food makes for a wonderful party, at the game or at home. Margaritas create instant cheer. Chili suffers no ills, and may even improve, if made ahead. Service is easy. I've even included a method of preserving the guacamole's color if you prefer to make it a day in advance.

If you like to serve margaritas in salted glasses, cut out a wedge of lime and run it around the rim of the glasses. Scatter the salt on wax paper and dip the wet rims into the salt. Stick the glasses in the freezer or ice chest for a few minutes to harden before pouring in the margaritas.

The chili is made with two kinds of chili powder—one for deeper flavor and the other for heat. Beer added to the chili disappears during cooking, but leaves behind a slight bitter edge and added depth of flavor.

If it's a cold day and you're lucky enough to be at the game, ladle or spoon the chili into oversize mugs from a wide-mouth thermos, leaving plenty of room for guests to heap on their own choice of garnishes. At home, serve buffet-style in large mugs or deep earthenware bowls.

Dessert, Mexican Hot Chocolate, is really a beverage—thick, rich, very chocolaty and doused with rum and Kahlúa. For those who never have enough to eat, you can offer tangerines—refreshing after the spicy food—and sugar cookies.

MARGARITAS BY THE BATCH

Makes about 1 quart

2 cups tequila
1 cup Triple Sec or other dry orange liqueur
1 cup freshly squeezed lime juice

1. Fill a large pitcher one-third to one-half full with ice. Pour in the tequila, Triple Sec and lime juice. Stir for a good 30 seconds.

2. Pour into iced (and salted if you wish) glasses or—for a tailgate—into a chilled thermos.

GUACAMOLE

This tangy avocado dip tastes best when freshly made. You can make it the day before, but if you do, guard against discoloration this way: Pack the guacamole into a bowl or container and smooth the top level. Mix 2 or 3 tablespoons of mayonnaise with 1 or 2 teaspoons of lemon juice to thin it. Spread this over the top of the guacamole. Before serving, stir the protective layer into the rest of the dip. Serve with tortilla chips or fresh vegetable sticks.

Makes about 2½ cups

1 garlic clove, split in half
2 large ripe avocados (The nubbly kind are best. The skins should be blackened, and they should feel like ripe peaches)
2 tablespoons fresh lemon juice
2 teaspoons grated onion
½ teaspoon salt
¼ teaspoon freshly ground black pepper
1 small jalapeño pepper, seeded and minced, or ⅛ teaspoon cayenne pepper, or more to taste
1 large tomato, peeled, seeded and finely diced

1. Rub a medium bowl with the cut garlic. Peel the avocados, remove the pits and mash the avocado coarsely in the bowl.

2. Add the lemon juice, onion, salt, black pepper and jalapeño and mix well. Taste and adjust the seasonings if necessary. Fold in the tomato, just until mixed.

SANTA FE CHILI

Beans in chili are largely a matter of personal taste. If you like them in, add 2 cups of cooked pinto beans to the finished chili and simmer for 5 minutes. I prefer mine without.

Whatever your preference, the dish becomes more festive when served with a variety of garnishes: chopped scallion or onion, sliced black olives, grated Cheddar cheese, sour cream. I like to put out a basket of warmed tortilla chips as well.

Pure ground chili powders are available in specialty shops and in some supermarkets.

Serves 6–8 (10 if you add the beans)

3 tablespoons vegetable oil
3 medium onions, chopped
3 large garlic cloves, finely chopped
3 pounds chuck steak, trimmed of excess fat
    and cut into ¼-inch dice
1½ teaspoons salt
¾ teaspoon freshly ground black pepper
3 tablespoons all-purpose flour
1½ cups (12 ounces) lager beer or water
3 tablespoons mild ground chiles
2 tablespoons hot ground chiles
2 teaspoons ground cumin
1 teaspoon oregano, crumbled
1 cup beef stock
1 can (28 ounces) Italian peeled tomatoes,
    with the liquid
2 cups cooked pinto beans (optional)

1. Heat the oil in a large flameproof casserole. Add the onions and sauté over moderately high heat, stirring occasionally, until beginning to brown, about 3 minutes. Add the garlic and sauté for 1 minute longer.

2. Add the beef and cook, stirring, until browned. Sprinkle the salt, pepper and flour over the meat and cook, stirring, for 1 to 2 minutes to cook the flour. Add the beer and bring to a boil, stirring to scrape up any browned bits from the bottom of the pan.

3. Season with the mild and hot chiles, the cumin and oregano. Add the stock and tomatoes with the liquid. Simmer over low heat, partially covered, stirring occasionally, for 1½ to 2 hours, until the meat is very tender and the sauce is thickened.

MEXICAN HOT CHOCOLATE

For a tailgate, make up a batch of this rich beverage and transport in a large thermos.

Makes 1 cup

2 teaspoons Dutch-process unsweetened
    cocoa powder
⅛ teaspoon ground cinnamon
½ cup boiling water
½ cup hot milk
2 tablespoons coffee liqueur, such as Kahlúa
    or Tia Maria

2 tablespoons amber rum, such as Mt. Gay
    or Appleton
⅛ teaspoon vanilla
1 cinnamon stick (about 2 inches long)

1. Place the cocoa and ground cinnamon in a large mug or heatproof glass. Gradually add the boiling water while stirring briskly to blend in the cocoa. Stir in the hot milk.

2. Add the coffee liqueur, rum and vanilla.

3. Garnish with a stick of cinnamon.

Garden Party

SPECIAL EQUIPMENT

1 ½ -quart thermos for soup

Thermos for iced tea

Large lidded bowl or serving
dish for chicken salad

Serving spoon for chicken salad

Basket for croissants

Mugs or soup bowls

Soup spoons (if you are using bowls)

Dessert forks

Cake server

Wineglasses

Cooler to carry chicken salad,
cake on plate and 2 to 3 bottles of
wine

This chic little luncheon would be as appropriate on the patio as in a rose arbor. It deserves fine china and silver, but tastes just as good on paper plates. If you have one of those beautiful picnic hampers with linen and utensils, this is the perfect menu with which to show it off.

The refreshing cucumber soup, a lovely pale green, is best served icy cold. Make it the day before and pour it into a chilled thermos just before leaving. Although the chicken salad can be made a day ahead, I prefer to poach the chicken and make the dressing ahead and to assemble the salad at the last moment so that the fruit remains as crisp as can be. It is a marvelous blend of fresh flavors. Serve it garnished with cherry tomatoes and a little watercress or Japanese radish sprouts for color. Buttery croissants are a wonderful accompaniment. A big rich California Chardonnay, such as Château St. Jean or Acacia, would go beautifully with this menu. The Chocolate Grand Mar-nier Cake speaks for itself. Carry it in a cooler to preserve the glaze, but take it out about 30 minutes before serving. An extra thermos filled with iced tea would be appropriate after this elegant meal.

COLD CUCUMBER-DILL SOUP

Serves 6

2 tablespoons vegetable oil
1 medium onion, chopped
2½ tablespoons all-purpose flour
1 can (13¾ ounces) chicken broth
2 cups water
2 large cucumbers, peeled, seeded and
  thickly sliced
Bouquet garni: 3 sprigs of parsley, 3 sprigs of
  dill, 6 peppercorns and ½ small bay leaf
  tied in a double thickness of cheesecloth
1 teaspoon salt
Dash of cayenne pepper
2 teaspoons fresh lemon juice
½ cup sour cream
2 tablespoons minced fresh dill and/or chives

1. In a large saucepan, heat the oil. Add the onion and cook over moderate heat, stirring occasionally, until soft and translucent, 3 to 5 minutes.

2. Add the flour and cook, stirring, for 2 minutes without letting the flour color to make a roux. Whisk in the chicken broth. Add the water and bring to a boil. Add the cucumbers, bouquet garni, salt and cayenne. Simmer, partially covered, until the cucumbers are soft, about 20 minutes.

3. Remove and discard the bouquet garni. Purée the soup, in batches if necessary, in a blender or food processor. Whisk in the lemon juice and sour cream. Taste and adjust the seasonings if necessary. The soup should be highly seasoned, as the flavors will mellow when chilled. Refrigerate in a tightly covered container. Serve as cold as possible, garnished with the fresh herbs.

CURRIED CHICKEN SALAD WITH HAM AND FRUITS

There must be as many kinds of chicken salad as there are people who love them. This recipe is particularly flavorful and appealing because it uses fruits that are available practically all year round. The fresh herbs used in the sauce—mint and basil—are now often available in supermarkets in winter as well as in summer. You can substitute a simple curry mayonnaise flavored with a little fresh lemon juice, but the taste will not be the same.

Serves 6–8

2 pounds chicken breasts, skinned and boned
Herbed Curry Sauce (recipe follows)
¼ pound Black Forest ham, sliced ¼ inch
    thick and cut into ¼-inch dice
1 Granny Smith or other tart apple, cored
    and cut into ½-inch dice
1 firm ripe pear, such as Anjou, cored and
    cut into ½-inch dice
1 cup diced fresh pineapple
½ cup finely diced red onion
½ cup toasted slivered almonds
½ cup raisins

1. In a large saucepan or heatproof casserole, poach the chicken breasts in salted water to cover over moderately low heat for 15 to 20 minutes, until white in the center but still juicy. Let cool to room temperature. Cut into 1-inch cubes.

2. In a large bowl, toss the chicken cubes with the Herbed Curry Sauce until evenly coated. Add the ham, apple, pear, pineapple, onion, almonds and raisins. Toss to mix. Cover and refrigerate until serving time.

HERBED CURRY SAUCE

Makes about 1 ⅓ cups

1 egg
1 tablespoon fresh lemon juice
1 teaspoon Dijon-style mustard
½ teaspoon salt
½ cup olive oil
½ cup safflower or corn oil
1 tablespoon white wine vinegar
¼ cup fresh basil leaves
2 tablespoons fresh mint leaves
¼ cup sour cream
1 tablespoon curry powder

1. In a blender or food processor, whirl the egg with the lemon juice, mustard and salt for about 5 seconds, until blended.

2. With the machine on, slowly drizzle in the olive and safflower oils. Add the vinegar, basil and mint and turn the machine on and off several times until the herbs are chopped.

3. Add the sour cream and curry powder and process until the sauce is blended and the herbs are finely minced. Cover and refrigerate until serving time.

CHOCOLATE GRAND MARNIER CAKE

Rich, dark and very chocolaty, this low moist cake is a European-style torte. It has very little flour and an equal amount of ground nuts. You cannot undercook it, but you can overcook it; so don't worry if the center is a little soft when it comes out of the oven. Don't be alarmed when this cake sinks a little while cooling. Like most chocolate cakes, it improves overnight.

Makes one 8-inch cake

1 ½ sticks (6 ounces) unsalted butter
6 ounces good-quality sweetened dark chocolate, such as Tobler Extra-Bittersweet or
   Lindt Excellence
½ cup sugar
4 eggs, separated
¼ cup Grand Marnier
1 teaspoon grated orange zest
1 teaspoon vanilla
¼ cup ground almonds
¼ cup cake flour
Pinch of salt

Chocolate Glaze

3 ounces good-quality dark sweetened chocolate, such as Tobler Extra-Bittersweet or Lindt Excellence
2 tablespoons Grand Marnier
3 tablespoons unsalted butter

1. Preheat the oven to 375°F. Butter an 8-inch springform pan about 2 inches deep. Line the bottom of the pan with a round of wax paper and butter the paper. Dust the entire pan with flour; tap out any excess.

2. In a small, heavy saucepan or in the top of a double boiler over hot water, melt the butter and chocolate together over low heat, stirring until smooth. Remove from the heat.

3. In a medium-size bowl, gradually beat the sugar into the egg yolks. Continue beating until the mixture is pale yellow and forms a ribbon. Beat in the Grand Marnier, orange zest and vanilla. Add the chocolate-butter mixture and the almonds; blend well. Add the flour and mix just until blended.

4. Beat the egg whites with the salt until stiff peaks form and the whites are still smooth and glossy but not dry. Add about one-fourth of the beaten whites to the chocolate batter and stir in to lighten the mixture. Scrape the batter into the bowl with the remaining egg whites and fold until no streaks of white remain. Turn into the prepared pan.

5. Bake for 20 to 22 minutes, until the edges are set and begin to pull away from the side of the pan. Let the cake rest for 5 to 10 minutes, then remove the side of the springform. Invert the cake onto a serving platter. Peel off the wax paper and let the cake cool completely before frosting.

6. To make the glaze, in a small heavy saucepan, melt the chocolate in the Grand Marnier over low heat, stirring until smooth.

7. Remove from the heat and stir in the butter, 1 tablespoon at a time, until blended and smooth. Cover the cake with a thin coating of this Chocolate Glaze.

Après Ski Party

SPECIAL EQUIPMENT

Mugs

2 serving dishes for ragout and rice

Large serving spoon for ragout

Serving spoons for rice and apples

This is hearty food for an active cold day. Whether your friends' or family's pleasure is cross-country skiing, downhill racing, sledding or simply a vigorous trek through the snow, you'll find this a comforting meal to return to.

The Broccoli and Cheese Soup can be made a day ahead, but do not add the Cheddar cheese until just before you serve it. Cheese can become tough upon prolonged contact with heat. The cheese can be carried in a separate container and stirred into each serving as the soup is poured.

Creole Port Ragout, a spicy tomatoey stew crunchy with green bell peppers, served on a bed of steamed rice, is highly seasoned with hot pepper sauce, Worcestershire and lemon juice, typical of Louisiana Creole cuisine. Maple Baked Apples with walnuts and dates, served at "room" temperature, which means either indoor room temperature or chilled according to the weather, makes a satisfyingly sweet seasonal end to this meal. Pass heavy cream separately if you wish.

For beverages, start with Hot Mulled Wine, one of my favorite cold-weather drinks, spiced with cinnamon and cloves, laced with brandy and served in large mugs. It is guaranteed to warm inside and out.

HOT MULLED WINE

With all the flavorings and spices, you don't need to use an expensive wine for this drink. I use a full-flavored jug wine.

Makes about 9 cups

½ gallon dry red wine, preferably a hearty
    Burgundy
2 cinnamon sticks
6 whole cloves
3 allspice berries, or ⅛ teaspoon ground
    allspice
¼ cup sugar
½ orange
½ lemon
½ cup brandy

1. In a large nonaluminum saucepan, combine the wine, cinnamon, cloves, allspice and sugar. Squeeze the juice of the orange half into the pan and toss in the rind. Do the same with the lemon.

2. Heat slowly, stirring occasionally to dissolve the sugar. Let the wine steep without boiling for 10 to 15 minutes.

3. Remove from the heat and add the brandy. Strain into a large thermos or into mugs to serve.

BROCCOLI AND CHEESE SOUP

Serves 6–8

1 large bunch of broccoli (1½ to 2 pounds)
2 tablespoons unsalted butter
1 tablespoon olive oil
2 medium onions, sliced
2 garlic cloves, coarsely chopped
2 tablespoons all-purpose flour
6 cups homemade chicken stock, or 2 cans
    (13¾ ounces each) chicken broth plus 2
    cups water
¼ cup heavy cream
1 tablespoon fresh lemon juice
1 teaspoon Worcestershire sauce
⅛ to ¼ teaspoon Tabasco sauce, to taste
¼ pound sharp Cheddar cheese, grated
    (1 cup)
Salt and freshly ground pepper

1. Trim off the ends of the broccoli stems. Remove and reserve any fresh green leaves. Peel the thick stalks and slice them into 1-inch pieces. Separate the florets into 1-inch pieces.

2. In a large saucepan or flameproof casserole, melt the butter in the oil over moderate heat. Add the onions and sauté until softened but not browned, about 3 minutes. Add the garlic and cook for 1 minute longer. Sprinkle on the flour and cook, stirring, without coloring for 1 to 2 minutes.

3. Add the stock and bring to a boil over moderately high heat. Add the broccoli stems to the stock and boil for 5 minutes. Add the florets and leaves and cook until the florets are tender but still bright green, about 3 minutes. Remove from the heat.

4. Let the soup cool slightly, then purée in batches in a blender or food processor. Return to the saucepan.

5. Add the cream, lemon juice, Worcestershire sauce and Tabasco. Simmer uncovered for 3 to 5 minutes, until heated through.

6. Just before serving, stir in the cheese. Season with salt and pepper if needed.

CREOLE PORK RAGOUT

Serves 6

3 pounds pork shoulder, trimmed of excess
    fat and cut into 1-inch squares about ½
    inch thick
1 teaspoon salt
½ teaspoon freshly ground pepper
6 tablespoons vegetable oil
2 large onions, sliced
1 cup dry white wine
1 can (35 ounces) Italian-style peeled toma-
    toes, with the juices reserved
1 garlic clove, crushed through a press
1 teaspoon marjoram
1 bay leaf
3 to 4 tablespoons lemon juice
1½ tablespoons Worcestershire sauce
½ teaspoon sugar
¼ to ½ teaspoon Tabasco sauce, to taste
2 medium-size green bell peppers, cut into
    1½-inch strips about ⅜ inch wide

1. Toss the pork pieces with the salt and pepper and set aside.

2. In a large flameproof casserole, heat 2 tablespoons of the oil. Add the onions and cook over moderately high heat, stirring occasionally, until they begin to brown, about 5 minutes. Remove from the heat.

3. In a large skillet, heat 2 tablespoons of the oil. Add as much of the pork as will fit easily in a single layer and sauté over moderately high heat, turning until pork is lightly browned all over, about 2 minutes. As the pieces brown, transfer them to the casserole with tongs or a slotted spoon. Repeat until all the meat is browned.

4. Pour off the fat from the skillet. Add the wine and bring to a boil, scraping the bottom with a wooden spoon to incorporate all the browned bits stuck to the pan. Add this liquid to the casserole.

5. Add the tomatoes and the juices, the garlic, marjoram, bay leaf, 2 tablespoons of the lemon juice, the Worcestershire sauce, sugar and Tabasco.

6. Bring to a boil, reduce the heat to a simmer and cook, covered, for 45 minutes, stirring occasionally. Uncover and cook until the meat is tender and the liquid reduced to a fairly thick sauce, 30 to 45 minutes longer. If the sauce is very thin, boil uncovered over moderately high heat, stirring frequently, until the sauce is reduced.

7. In a large skillet, heat the remaining 2 tablespoons oil. Add the green peppers and sauté over moderate heat, stirring frequently, until they are softened but still have a slight crunch, about 5 minutes. With a slotted spoon, transfer the peppers to the ragout.

8. Simmer uncovered for 5 to 10 minutes. Taste the sauce and add up to 2 tablespoons more lemon juice, to taste. The flavor should be tangy and piquant. Season with salt, pepper and additional Tabasco. Serve over steamed rice.

MAPLE BAKED APPLES

For this recipe, use a flavorful baking apple that will hold its shape, such as a Cortland or Rome Beauty. Yellow Delicious also work well. I like these maple-flavored apples as is, with just a moistening of the pan juices, but they can be served with a pitcher of heavy cream on the side.

Serves 6

6 medium baking apples, such as Cortland, Rome Beauty or Yellow Delicious
6 tablespoons chopped walnuts
6 tablespoons chopped dates
¾ teaspoon cinnamon
3 tablespoons maple syrup
2 tablespoons unsalted butter

1. Preheat the oven to 375°F. Core each apple to within ½ inch of the bottom. Peel off the top third of the skin. Using a grapefruit knife or small spoon, scoop out the apple, leaving a ½-inch shell. Coarsely chop and reserve half of the removed apple; discard the remainder.

2. In a small bowl, toss the walnuts, dates, cinnamon and reserved chopped apple to mix. Fill each apple with about 2 tablespoons of the walnut-date mixture. Pour ½ tablespoon maple syrup into each apple and top each with 1 teaspoon butter.

3. Place the apples in a baking dish filled with about ½ inch of water. Bake for about 40 minutes, basting frequently with the pan juices, until the apples are soft but still hold their shape. Serve warm, at room temperature or chilled, with some of the pan juices spooned over them.

Horse Show

MENU

Serves 6

Crudités with Creamy Herb Dip*

Shrimp Bisque with Fennel*

Duck Pâté

Assorted Mustards

Tomato, Arugula and Mushroom Salad
with Oil and Vinegar

Crusty French Bread

Stilton and Pears

Bread Pudding*

SPECIAL EQUIPMENT

Large, medium-size and small covered containers for *crudités*, salad and dip

Tightly lidded jar for vinaigrette

Tightly lidded jar for cream

Thermos and mugs for shrimp bisque

Corkscrew

Large picnic hamper

Wineglasses

Horse trials take place virtually year round, but the most popular horse shows are in spring and fall. This elegant, yet easy-to-assemble menu works best in either early spring or the cooler part of autumn, when appetites are stimulated by the crisp, seasonal weather.

Start with raw vegetables and a Creamy Herb Dip. Choose produce with an eye to the season. Along with the standard broccoli, carrots, peppers, and zucchini, in spring add fresh baby asparagus, briefly blanched in boiling water to tenderize and set the color yet maintain enough firmness for dipping. Sugarsnap or snow peas and baby radishes are delicious in early summer. In fall, cherry tomatoes are at their peak, as are Belgian endive and kirby cucumbers.

Shrimp Bisque with Fennel, carried in a thermos, is rich and creamy. A thick soup, it is best eaten with soup spoons from cups or small mugs; but it can be drunk. Duck pâté is easily purchased at a food specialty shop, but you can substitute a country-style or liver pâté if you prefer. Serve an interesting variety of mustards—green peppercorn, grainy, Dijon, tarragon. Unless the day is very cold, carry the pâté in a small cooler to be safe. Also pack the cream to serve with

dessert and, if it is a warm day, the *crudités*. Serve the salad and bread along with the pâté. Stilton cheese and pears, transported at room temperature, add another elegant touch, especially if offered with a glass of vintage port. Bread pudding, served on dessert plates or in shallow bowls, is immensely satisfying and sweetly delicious.

CREAMY HERB DIP

Makes about 1 ¼ cups

4 ounces cream cheese, softened
⅓ cup mayonnaise
1 tablespoon fresh lemon juice
1 garlic clove, crushed through a press
¼ teaspoon dry mustard
¼ teaspoon thyme
Dash of cayenne pepper
1 tablespoon minced chives
1 tablespoon minced fresh dill, or 1 teaspoon
    dried dillweed
Salt and freshly ground pepper

1. In a small bowl, blend together the cream cheese and mayonnaise until smooth. Gradually stir in the lemon juice.

2. Add the garlic, mustard, thyme and cayenne. Mix well. Stir in the chives and dill. Season with salt and freshly ground pepper to taste.

SHRIMP BISQUE WITH FENNEL

Serve this creamy rich soup in large mugs. In summer, omit the butter at the end, refrigerate and serve chilled.

Serves 6

2 tablespoons vegetable oil
1 large leek (white and tender green), well rinsed and sliced (to yield about 1½ cups)
1 large fennel bulb (plus about 2 inches of the stalks), halved and sliced
2½ tablespoons all-purpose flour
½ cup dry white wine
5 cups water
1 tablespoon tomato paste
1½ teaspoons salt
¼ teaspoon white pepper
Dash of cayenne pepper
1 pound medium shrimp, shelled and deveined
1 cup heavy cream
⅓ cup Pernod
1 tablespoon fresh lemon juice
3 tablespoons unsalted butter

1. In a large flameproof casserole or saucepan, heat the oil. Add the leek and sauté, stirring, over moderately high heat for 2 minutes, without allowing it to brown. Add the fennel, reduce the heat to moderate, cover and cook, stirring occasionally, until the vegetables are softened but not browned, 10 to 15 minutes.

2. Sprinkle the flour over the vegetables and cook, stirring, for 2 minutes without letting the flour color. Whisk in the white wine. Add the water, tomato paste, salt, white pepper and cayenne. Simmer, partially covered, for 30 to 40 minutes, until the fennel is quite soft.

3. Add the shrimp and cook for 1 minute; immediately remove from the heat. Stir in the cream.

4. Purée the soup in batches. Strain back into the pan. Heat through. Add the Pernod, lemon juice and butter just before serving or before pouring into a thermos.

BREAD PUDDING

Serves 6–8

⅓ cup currants or raisins
¼ cup amber rum, such as Appleton or Mt.
    Gay, or dark rum, such as Myers
½ pound challah (egg bread), cut into ⅜-
    inch-thick slices
3 tablespoons unsalted butter, at room
    temperature
2¼ cups milk
2 whole eggs
3 egg yolks
¾ cup sugar
1½ teaspoons vanilla
Heavy cream

1. In a small bowl, macerate the currants in the rum for at least 15 minutes.

2. Preheat the oven to 350°F. Trim most of the crust off the bread. Lightly butter both sides of the bread slices and place them on a baking sheet. Bake, turning once, until the bread is lightly toasted, 5 to 10 minutes. Remove the bread from the oven but leave the oven on.

3. Arrange the bread in a buttered 9-inch oval gratin dish or in an 8-inch-square baking pan, overlapping the slices as necessary. Drain the currants, reserving the rum. Sprinkle the currants over the bread.

4. Heat the milk in a medium-size saucepan until bubbles form around the rim. Remove from the heat.

5. In a large bowl, whisk the whole eggs and egg yolks with the sugar until pale in color and thickened. Gradually whisk the hot milk into the egg mixture. Beat in the vanilla and reserved rum. Pour this custard over the bread.

6. Place the gratin dish in a deep roasting pan on the middle rack of the oven. Add enough hot water to the roaster to reach halfway up the side of the gratin dish. Bake for about 30 minutes, until the custard is set.

7. Remove the bread pudding from its water bath and let cool. Serve warm, at room temperature, or slightly chilled, with a pitcher of cream on the side.

Autumn Leaves

SPECIAL EQUIPMENT

1-gallon thermos or hot-beverage jug
for mulled cider

Mugs for hot cider

Small covered container for mixed
nuts

2 medium-size covered containers
for salads

Basket for muffins

2 large serving spoons

1 serving fork

Pie server

Large picnic hamper

Fall is an invigorating season. Those brilliant blue cloudless skies, slashed with the copper color of the leaves, make me want to jump in a car and drive. Whether it is just to view the magnificent foliage or it turns into a stop-and-go day of antiquing, it's fun to share a day's outing with friends, piled into one car or in a caravan. This menu is equally appropriate for such a group of adults or for a family outing. Lay out the spread on a tartan blanket if you have one. Use a basket of colorful leaves or pine cones, gathered before eating, as a centerpiece.

Fresh cider is one of autumn's seasonal delights not to be missed. That refreshing, just-pressed tang bears about as much resemblance to the cloying processed bottled cider as fresh asparagus does to canned. If you have a farmer's market or cider mill near you, go for it. If not, look for fresh cider in the fruit and vegetable section of your supermarket. Fresh cider turns to vinegar quickly, so be sure to refrigerate it when you get home and use as soon as possible.

While you are laying out the feast, pass a bowl of mixed nuts. Whether you are serving baked ham or smoked pork, have it sliced for you or slice it at home; allow ⅓ pound per person. Bring an assortment of mustards, such as Dijon, green peppercorn, Pommery. Tangy Orange-Radish Salad, a beautiful mix of orange and red, is refreshing with the smoked meat. Cheddar Cornbread Muffins, spiked with hot pepper, make an irresistible accompaniment. If you end up with a large crowd and want to put out a larger spread, tack on potato or macaroni salad, either store-bought or homemade (Old-Fashioned Potato Salad, page 82; Quick Macaroni Salad, page 63).

For dessert, Bourbon Sweet-Potato Pie is substantial and even better if made a day or two ahead. It can be served on plates and eaten with a fork, but, in a pinch, is sturdy enough to eat out of hand with a napkin. Be sure to bring a thermos of hot coffee.

HOT MULLED CIDER

Makes about 8 cups

½ gallon fresh apple cider
3 cinnamon sticks, split lengthwise and then again crosswise in half
6 whole cloves
3 allspice berries, or ⅛ teaspoon ground allspice
⅛ to ¼ teaspoon ground cinnamon (optional)

1. In a large nonaluminum saucepan, combine the cider, cinnamon sticks, cloves and allspice. Bring to just below a simmer, reduce the heat to very low and let steep for 20 minutes.

2. Taste; if the cinnamon flavor is not strong enough, add the ground cinnamon.

ORANGE-RADISH SALAD

James Beard introduced me to this refreshing combination of flavors in my first cooking course.

Serves 4–6

5 navel oranges
12 radishes, sliced
1½ tablespoons chopped scallion
2 tablespoons olive oil
1 tablespoon fresh lemon juice
¼ teaspoon salt
¼ teaspoon sugar

1. With a small, sharp paring knife, cut the peel and white pith off the oranges. Cut the oranges into thick slices and then quarter the slices. Place in a bowl. Add the radishes and scallion.

2. In a small jar, combine the olive oil, lemon juice, salt and sugar. Shake to blend and dissolve the sugar. Just before serving, pour over the salad and toss.

CHEDDAR CORNBREAD MUFFINS

Makes 12

1 cup all-purpose flour
1 cup yellow cornmeal
3 teaspoons baking powder
½ teaspoon salt
⅛ teaspoon freshly ground black pepper
⅛ teaspoon cayenne pepper
1 cup (lightly packed) grated or finely
    shredded sharp Cheddar cheese
1 egg
1 cup milk
4 tablespoons unsalted butter, melted and
    cooled slightly

1. Preheat the oven to 400°F. Butter a 12 2½-inch muffin tin.

2. Into a large bowl, sift together the flour, cornmeal, baking powder, salt, black pepper and cayenne. Add the cheese and toss lightly.

3. In a small bowl, beat the egg lightly. Beat in the milk and butter. Pour this liquid into the dry ingredients and quickly stir 3 or 4 times around the bowl with a folding motion. Do not overmix; the batter should be lumpy. Spoon into the prepared muffin tin.

4. Bake for 20 to 22 minutes, until the muffins are golden brown and a tester inserted in the center comes out clean.

BOURBON-SWEET POTATO PIE

Makes one 9-inch pie

⅓ cup (packed) golden raisins
¼ cup bourbon
2 tablespoons melted butter
2 large sweet potatoes or yams, cooked and
    mashed (to yield about 2 cups purée)
2 eggs, lightly beaten
⅔ cup dark brown sugar
¾ cup hot milk
1 teaspoon vanilla
1¼ teaspoons cinnamon
½ teaspoon nutmeg
½ teaspoon salt
½ cup chopped pecans (optional)
Unbaked 9-inch Pie Shell (recipe follows)

1. Preheat the oven to 450°F. Soak the raisins in the bourbon for at least 30 minutes.

2. Beat the butter into the sweet potato purée. Beat in the eggs, brown sugar, milk, vanilla, cinnamon, nutmeg and salt. Mix in the raisins and bourbon and the pecans if you are adding them. Turn into the unbaked pie shell.

3. Bake the pie for 15 minutes. Reduce the oven temperature to 350°F. and continue to bake for 30 to 40 minutes longer, until the crust is golden brown and a knife inserted in the center of the pie comes out clean. Let cool before serving.

UNBAKED 9-INCH PIE SHELL

1½ cups all-purpose flour
½ teaspoon salt
6 tablespoons butter, cut into small bits
2 tablespoons vegetable shortening
3 to 4 tablespoons cold water

1. In a medium-size bowl, combine the flour and salt. Cut in the butter and shortening until the mixture resembles coarse meal. (I like to do this with my fingertips, using quick pinching/smearing motions.) Toss with 3 tablespoons of the water and press into a ball. If a lot of crumbs remain on the bottom of the bowl and the dough does not mass together, add the remaining tablespoon of water, 1 teaspoon at a time, until it does. Press into a 6-inch disk, wrap in wax paper, place in a plastic bag and refrigerate for at least 30 minutes.

2. On a lightly floured surface, roll out the dough to about a 12-inch round ⅛ inch thick. Fit into a 9-inch pie pan. Trim the edges, leaving a ½-inch overhang. Fold over the excess dough; pinch and crimp the edges decoratively. Prick all over with a fork. Refrigerate for at least 30 minutes before baking.

A Day at the Races

MENU

Serves 6

Iced Vodka

Oysters on the Half Shell

Smoked Salmon Canapés*

Chicken Medallions with Leeks and
Shiitake Mushrooms*

Wild Rice Salad*

Belgian Endive and Bibb Lettuce
with Walnuts and Goat Cheese

Quick Strawberry Shortcake*

SPECIAL EQUIPMENT

Large cooler with lots of ice to hold
bottle of vodka, salmon canapés,
chicken medallions and cake, all in
their own containers

Separate small chest to hold oysters
on the half shell over ice

Covered containers for canapés,
chicken, rice salad and green salad
with cheese

Small tightly lidded container for
salad dressing

Domed cake carrier for strawberry
shortcake

Small glasses for vodka

Trays for oysters and canapés

Bowl for lemon wedges

Large picnic hamper

Classic horse racing has a tradition of lavish food and entertaining associated with it. In Charlottesville, Virginia, the scene of many a summer horse race, the track parking lot is the scene for hundreds of tailgates, with nary a hotdog in sight. Southern specialties abound—fancy cakes, biscuits with homemade jams and jellies, Southern fried chicken, wild duck, shrimp, pickled beets and cucumbers and salads galore. Champagne and mint juleps vie for frosted glasses.

Here is a manageable yet extremely elegant tailgate for early summer. Start with iced vodka, left overnight in the freezer and carried in an ice chest so it is syrupy when poured. A twist of orange or lemon peel is the most it needs. Unless someone in your party is expert at shucking oysters and a good sport, have the oysters freshly shucked for you; pick them up on the way if possible. Ask your fish market to pack them for you on the half shell over ice. Don't accept them swimming in their own liquor with the shells on the side; the texture and flavor will not be the same. Allow 6 to 12 oysters per person. Bring along plenty of lemon wedges and cocktail napkins. Smoked Salmon Canapés, flavored with a touch of lemon, capers and fresh dill, are another elegant appetizer, sublime with the iced vodka.

When you are ready, move leisurely on to a sumptuous meal of tender chicken medallions, filled with leeks and shiitake mushrooms. I like to serve these with a lemon mayonnaise lightened with a touch of whipped cream. Wild Rice Salad, crunchy with water chestnuts, enlivened with scallions and Black Forest ham, also has a subtle Oriental touch in the sesame oil and rice vinegar dressing.

Follow with a salad of Belgian endive and Bibb lettuce, dressed with good oil and vinegar, sprinkled with chopped walnuts and served with crumbled goat cheese. Assemble the salad with the walnuts and cheese at home. Carry the dressing separately and toss shortly before serving.

Dessert is Quick Strawberry Shortcake, made from store-bought pound cake, but dressed up to look like a fancy torte. If you make the whipped cream in a food processor so that it is dense (see Note, page 49), you can even assemble this pretty confection the night before. Or throw it together in the 10 to 15 minutes it will take before you leave the house. Pack the strawberry shortcake on a platter. Either encase the platter and cake with aluminum foil, avoiding touching the sides of the cake, or set the cake and platter in a larger plastic container with a lid or under a plastic domed cake carrier. Transport it in a cooler with an ice pack or in an ice chest to preserve the whipped cream.

SMOKED SALMON CANAPES

For a tailgate, make the cream cheese spread the night before. In the morning, assemble the canapés. Transport these open-faced sandwiches in a tightly covered container, with sheets of wax paper between the layers, in a cooler. Remove them about half an hour before serving.

Makes 20 pieces

4 ounces cream cheese, at room temperature
4 tablespoons unsalted butter, at room temperature
1½ tablespoons minced fresh dill
1 tablespoon minced fresh chives
2 teaspoons fresh lemon juice
1½ teaspoons capers, rinsed, drained and finely chopped
¼ teaspoon coarsely ground pepper
Dash of Tabasco sauce
Pinch of salt
5 slices of thinly sliced, square, Danish-style pumpernickel bread
¼ pound thinly sliced smoked salmon, preferably Norwegian or Scotch
Sprigs of fresh dill, for garnish

1. In a small bowl, mix the cream cheese and butter until well blended. Add the dill and chives. Gradually stir in the lemon juice. Season with the capers, pepper, Tabasco and salt. Cover and refrigerate until several hours before you plan to serve the canapés. This mixture will keep well overnight.

2. Spread a thin layer of the cream cheese mixture over the bread slices, covering to the very edges of the bread. Top with a single layer of salmon, patching where necessary. Cut each slice of bread twice diagonally into 4 small triangles. Top each canapé with a small sprig of dill. Cover and refrigerate, if desired, for up to 4 hours before serving.

CHICKEN MEDALLIONS WITH LEEKS & SHIITAKE MUSHROOMS

These attractive medallions are best if cooked until barely done and still juicy. They will finish cooking off heat. I like to serve them at room temperature with a lemon-flavored homemade mayonnaise.

Serves 6

6 good-sized skinless, boneless chicken breast
    halves
2 tablespoons light olive oil
2 tablespoons fresh lemon juice
1 onion, thinly sliced
12 sprigs of parsley with stems
12 medium dried shiitake mushrooms
12 leek greens, cut into 6-inch lengths
Salt and freshly ground pepper
3 tablespoons unsalted butter

1. If you have time, sprinkle the chicken breasts with the oil and lemon juice, layer them with the onion slices and parsley and let them marinate at room temperature for 1 hour. (This is from the great chef Escoffier; it adds a lovely flavor to the chicken, but it is not essential.) If time is short, pat the chicken breasts dry and begin with Step 2.

2. Place the dried mushrooms in a bowl and cover with boiling water. Let soak until soft, 20 to 30 minutes. Squeeze the mushrooms dry. Cut off and discard the stems. Quarter or halve the caps.

3. Dip the leek greens into a pot of boiling water for about 30 seconds, until softened but still bright green. Rinse briefly under cold running water and drain on paper towels.

4. Place the chicken breasts between 2 sheets of wax paper and pound them to flatten them evenly into rough rectangles. Season on both sides with salt and pepper.

5. To assemble, lay each chicken breast smooth side down, with a long side nearest to you. Cover with 2 lengths of leek green. Arrange the shiitake mushrooms along the longer edge of the breast near you. Roll up each chicken piece so that the mushrooms and leeks are spiraled in the center.

6. Melt the butter in a large skillet over moderately high heat. Add the rolled chicken breasts, seam side down. Sauté them, turning, until lightly browned all over, about 3 minutes. Reduce the heat to low, cover and cook, turning once, until just cooked through, about 5 minutes. Remove from the pan and let stand for 5 to 10 minutes before slicing crosswise into ½-inch medallions. Serve warm or at room temperature.

WILD RICE SALAD

This tasty rice salad is perfect for any picnic or buffet. It can be made a day ahead and held, covered, in the refrigerator, though I like to add the scallions the same day I plan to serve. This salad does not need to be transported in a cooler and is best at room temperature.

Serves 6

1 can (13¾ ounces) chicken broth
⅔ cup wild rice, well rinsed
⅔ cup Converted long-grain white rice
1 teaspoon sugar
¼ cup rice wine vinegar
3 tablespoons Oriental sesame oil
Several dashes of Tabasco sauce, or more to taste
¾ cup diced cooked ham (I like to use Black Forest or a flavorful baked ham)
½ cup diced water chestnuts
2 scallions, thinly sliced

1. In a medium-size saucepan, bring the chicken broth to a boil with 1½ cups of water. Add the wild rice, cover tightly and cook for about 35 minutes, until the rice is tender but still slightly resistant to the bite. The liquid will not all be absorbed, so begin tasting after 30 minutes. Drain and rinse briefly under cold running water; drain well. Place in a large bowl.

2. Meanwhile, cook the Converted rice in 1½ cups of boiling salted water until the liquid is absorbed and the rice is tender, 20 to 25 minutes. Rinse briefly under cold running water; drain well. Add to the wild rice.

3. Dissolve the sugar in the rice wine vinegar and pour over the warm rice. Toss well. Add the sesame oil and Tabasco and toss again. Let stand for about 15 minutes, tossing occasionally.

4. Add the ham, water chestnuts and scallions and toss to mix. Serve at room temperature.

QUICK STRAWBERRY SHORTCAKE

Serves 6–8

1 pound cake, 10 to 14 ounces
4 tablespoons kirsch or Grand Marnier
1½ cups heavy cream
1½ tablespoons confectioners' sugar
1 teaspoon vanilla
2 tablespoons seedless red raspberry jam
1½ pints strawberries, halved if large

1. Trim the brown crust off the top of the cake to level it. Cut the cake horizontally into 4 even layers. Sprinkle ½ tablespoon kirsch over each layer.

2. Beat the cream until soft peaks form. Add the confectioners' sugar, vanilla and remaining 1½ tablespoons kirsch and beat until stiff.

3. To assemble the cake, line up two of the cake layers, moistened sides up, long sides together, on a serving platter to make a square cake. Spread the raspberry jam over the cake. Cover with about one-third of the whipped cream and cover completely with strawberries. Place the remaining two cake layers on top, moistened sides up. Frost the top and sides of the cake with the remaining whipped cream. Decorate the top with the remaining berries. To serve, cut into rectangular pieces.

Note Whipped cream made in a food processor is denser but will hold up longer than beaten whipped cream. Turn on the machine and pour the cream in slowly through the feed tube. Continue to process for 10 to 20 seconds until soft peaks form. Add the confectioners' sugar, kirsch and vanilla and process until stiff; do not overprocess or the cream will turn into butter.

Regatta Tailgate

MENU

Serves 6

Sesame-Cheese Biscuits*

Iced Beet Soup*

Lemon and Lime Seafood Salad*

Zucchini Barquettes with
Tabbouleh*

Stilton and Pears

Mixed Berries and Cream

SPECIAL EQUIPMENT

Large covered container for seafood
salad

Shallow flat-bottomed container with
lid for zucchini barquettes

Small covered container for extra
tabbouleh

Covered container lined with paper
towels for rinsed and drained berries

Linen-lined basket for sesame
crackers (can double for crackers
with cheese)

Tightly lidded jar or unopened
container of cream

Cheeseboard or plate and cheese
spreader

Small pitcher for cream

Small jar of sugar

Medium-size cooler

In Henley, England, the sculling regattas on the Thames River offer an excuse for loyal British subjects to pack their Jaguars and Bentleys with the best china and cut crystal. Folding tea tables are covered with heirloom lace cloths and set with ornate silver.

Here in America, Newport, Rhode Island, has been the scene of the grand America's Cup yacht race in recent years. On-shore spectators and boating enthusiasts have watched patiently as the graceful 12-Meters went billowing back and forth across the horizon. Every Sunday sailor knows the pleasure of a race and the breathtaking sight of myriad white sails against the sparkling sea.

This is a stylish menu to honor the

noble sport. It is fit for a yacht or a well-set table along the shore. Begin over cocktails with Sesame-Cheese Biscuits, buttery and crumbly, with a pleasant peppery bite. Deep red Iced Beet Soup, served with an attractive garniture of sour cream, cucumber and dill, is thin and clear, with intense flavor. It can be served hot, but I prefer it well chilled, especially in summer. This soup can be made well ahead and refrigerated or frozen; it freezes perfectly. Ladle into bowls or pour into mugs or cups.

Lemon and Lime Seafood Salad, made with scallops, shrimp and squid, is a delightfully refreshing dish for a summer afternoon. It can be made a day or two ahead. Carry it in a tightly lidded container in your ice chest or cooler. Let warm slightly before serving. Tabbouleh is an out-of-the-ordinary accompaniment, nice when fresh mint is in season. Here it is attractively presented in scooped-out zucchini shells.

Either serve the Brie as a cheese course next, or follow the meal with the dessert of berries and cream and put out the cheese and crackers later in the afternoon, when appetites make their unexpected return.

SESAME-CHEESE BISCUITS

These are fabulous cocktail nibbles, perfect for parties, picnics and everyday snacking. They'll be snatched up as quickly as you serve them. They are simple to make. This dough cannot be overworked, and it rolls out easily between two sheets of wax paper.

Makes 4 to 5 dozen

½ stick (2 ounces) unsalted butter, at room temperature

2 ounces imported Parmesan cheese, grated
2 ounces sharp white Cheddar cheese, grated or finely shredded
¾ cup all-purpose flour
½ teaspoon salt
Large pinch of cayenne pepper, or to taste (I use a scant ⅛ teaspoon, but I like it *hot*)
1 egg yolk
Toasted sesame seeds (about ⅓ cup)

1. In a medium-size bowl, mash together the butter and cheeses with a wooden spoon. Gradually work in the flour, about one-third at a time. (Do not try to mix the dough completely with the spoon; the flour will bind, but the dough will be white in patches.) Blend in the salt and cayenne.

2. Knead the dough in the bowl with your hand, squeezing it between your fingers and blending until it is smooth and uniform and has lost its whitish appearance. Divide in half to make rolling out easier. Wrap well in plastic and refrigerate until chilled, at least 30 minutes or overnight.

3. Preheat the oven to 375°F. Remove one piece of dough from the refrigerator at a time. Let stand for 5 to 10 minutes to soften slightly. Then roll out between 2 sheets of waxed paper to a square or rectangle about ⅛ inch thick. Trim the edges evenly.

4. In a small bowl, beat the egg yolk with 1 tablespoon of water until blended to make an egg glaze. Brush the dough with a coating of the glaze. Sprinkle with half of the sesame seeds. Cut into 1½-inch squares and transfer with a spatula to a heavy baking sheet.

5. Bake the crackers for 12 minutes, or until pale golden. Repeat Steps 3 to 5 with the remaining dough.

ICED BEET SOUP

Makes about 1 quart

2 bunches of beets, preferably small (about 2½ pounds trimmed), peeled and coarsely chopped
1 large onion, coarsely chopped
1 large carrot, peeled and coarsely chopped
1 large tomato, coarsely chopped
1 can (13¾ ounces) chicken broth
2 tablespoons fresh lemon juice
1 teaspoon white wine vinegar
1 teaspoon sugar
½ teaspoon ground coriander
½ teaspoon salt
⅛ teaspoon freshly ground pepper
Sour cream
Chopped cucumber
Minced fresh dill

1. In a large nonaluminum saucepan, combine the beets, onion, carrot, tomato and chicken broth with 6 cups of water. Bring to a boil, reduce the heat and simmer, partially covered, for 1 hour.

2. Strain the soup through a fine mesh sieve, pressing on the vegetables to extract as much flavor as possible. Discard the vegetables. Season the soup with the lemon juice, vinegar, sugar, coriander, salt and pepper. Let cool; then cover and refrigerate for at least 4 hours and preferably overnight, until thoroughly chilled.

3. Serve cold, garnished with a dollop of sour cream and a sprinkling of chopped cucumber and dill.

LEMON AND LIME SEAFOOD SALAD

The only trick in this delicious simple salad is not to overcook the seafood. Perfectly done, the shrimp and scallops will be just opaque in the center, succulent and flavorful. The squid will be tender but not rubbery.

Serves 6

Court Bouillon

2½ quarts water
1 celery rib with leaves, quartered
1 carrot, quartered
1 onion, quartered
6 parsley stems
1 imported bay leaf
8 or 10 black peppercorns
2 tablespoons white wine vinegar
1 teaspoon salt

Seafood Salad

¾ pound sea scallops, cut into halves
¾ pound medium shrimp, shelled and deveined
1 pound cleaned squid, bodies cut into rings, tentacles halved or quartered lengthwise
⅓ cup fresh lime juice
3½ tablespoons fresh lemon juice
⅓ cup olive oil, preferably extra-virgin
1 small garlic clove, crushed through a press

¼ teaspoon salt
¼ teaspoon freshly ground pepper
¼ cup chopped flat-leaf parsley
Lemon and lime slices, for garnish

1. Bring all the court bouillon ingredients to a boil in a large nonaluminum saucepan. Reduce the heat to moderately low and simmer, uncovered, for 15 minutes. Strain out the solids and return the liquid to the pan.

2. Bring the strained court bouillon to a boil over moderately high heat. Add the scallops and simmer for 1½ minutes, or until they are barely opaque in the center. Quickly remove them with a large strainer or strain over a bowl to catch the liquid. Put the scallops in a large bowl. Return the liquid to the saucepan.

3. Add the shrimp and cook for about 1 minute. The shrimp are done when they are pink and loosely curled. Remove or strain them as described in Step 2. Add the shrimp to the scallops and return the liquid to a boil.

4. Add the squid, reduce the heat to moderately low and boil slowly for 20 to 30 minutes, until tender.

5. Meanwhile, toss the warm scallops and shrimp with the lime juice, lemon juice and olive oil.

6. When the squid is done, drain well and add to the other seafood. Add the garlic, salt, pepper and parsley and toss well. Cover and refrigerate for at least 2 hours or overnight.

(This salad keeps well for up to 2 days.) Garnish with slices of lemon and lime before serving.

ZUCCHINI BARQUETTES WITH TABBOULEH

To transport this dish, either wrap the zucchini, carry the tabbouleh in a covered container and assemble at the picnic site; or fill the barquettes at home and wrap tightly in a single layer. Pack the extra tabbouleh separately.

Serves 6

3 zucchini (7 to 8 inches long)
Salt and freshly ground black pepper
2 tablespoons red wine vinegar
2 tablespoons olive oil
Tabbouleh (see page 87)

1. Trim the stem ends off the zucchini and slice off just the brown tip at the bottom. Cut the zucchini lengthwise into halves.

2. Bring a large pot of salted water to a boil. Add the zucchini and cook for 3 to 5 minutes, until tender but still firm. Drain and rinse under cold running water.

3. With a spoon, scoop out the inside of each zucchini half, leaving a ¼-inch "barquette" shell all around. Season the insides of the barquettes lightly with salt and pepper. Sprinkle each with 1 teaspoon vinegar and 1 teaspoon oil.

4. To serve, fill the barquettes with about half the tabbouleh, mounding them in the center. Pass the remaining tabbouleh separately.

QUICK AND EASY PICNICS

Sailing Lunch

SPECIAL EQUIPMENT

Large thermos for soup

Bowls and spoons or cups for soup

Bowls for pickles, tomatoes and
olives

I learned the hard way that aboard a moving vessel food is best kept simple and easy to prepare. It must be hearty enough to satisfy the ever-present craving for food that seems to be present at sea and the outrageous appetites stimulated by the brisk winds and hard muscle work of sailing. Yet I am always determined that my crew dines well and with at least a suggestion of elegance.

This menu is particularly easy on the galley slave. Though the lentil soup can be made on board, under sail, as I've done many times, it is easily prepared ahead and carried in a heated thermos or two. I thin it to drinking consistency and serve it in large mugs filled only half to two-thirds of the way up. Everyone is welcome to seconds or thirds, but small portions in large cups help ensure the soup will remain in the cup rather than land in your lap after an unexpected roll. Again, if you are cruising, sandwiches can be assembled in the galley, but for a day trip I prepare them at home before we leave. Spread the bread with Dijon-style or honey mustard and, for a very French touch, with sweet butter as well. A pickle or two and a few cherry tomatoes and olives on each plate lifts lunch from just a sandwich to epicurean fare.

LENTIL SOUP

When I make this on the boat, I call it Stone Soup, not only because the dried lentils look like tiny pebbles, but because the soup keeps on going and seems to yield something out of nothing. Leftovers are poured into a thermos for the night watch. Next day, whatever remains will have thickened considerably. I thin this concentrate with water, add more salt, pepper, vinegar and Tabasco sauce and serve it again; the crew loves it.

Serves 6–8

3 tablespoons olive oil
1 large onion, chopped
1 medium carrot, peeled and chopped
1 celery rib with leafy top, chopped
2 garlic cloves, minced
½ pound (1 cup) lentils, rinsed and picked over to remove any grit
2 smoked ham hocks
Bouquet garni: 4 parsley sprigs, ¼ teaspoon marjoram, 2 whole cloves, 1 small bay leaf and 8 peppercorns tied in a double thickness of cheesecloth
1 teaspoon salt
½ teaspoon freshly ground pepper
1½ tablespoons red wine vinegar

1 or 2 dashes of Tabasco sauce, to taste
2 tablespoons minced parsley

1. In a large saucepan, heat the oil. Add the onion and sauté over moderate heat, stirring occasionally, until onion is softened and beginning to color, about 5 minutes. Add the carrot and celery and sauté until the vegetables are softened and the onion is lightly browned, about 5 minutes longer. Add the garlic and sauté until fragrant but not brown, about 1 minute.

2. Add 6 cups of water and the lentils. Bury the ham hocks and the bouquet garni in the lentils. Add additional water to cover if necessary. Season with the salt and pepper. Bring to a boil, reduce the heat and simmer, covered, until the lentils are tender, 30 to 45 minutes.

3. Remove and discard the bouquet garni. Remove the ham hocks and set aside. With the back of a spoon, mash some of the lentils against the side of the pan to thicken the soup slightly.

4. As soon as the ham hocks are cool enough to handle, cut the meat off the bones; discard the bones. Cut the meat into small dice; return to the soup.

5. Reheat the soup if necessary. Season with the vinegar and Tabasco sauce. Taste and adjust the seasonings if necessary. Just before serving, stir in the minced parsley. Serve hot.

QUICK ZUCCHINI PICKLES

Makes 2 pints

1½ pounds small zucchini, 4 to 5 inches long
  (about 6)
1 medium onion, sliced
8 to 12 large sprigs of fresh dill
4 garlic cloves, bruised
2 small dried hot red peppers
¾ cup cider vinegar
3 tablespoons sugar
1 teaspoon salt

DILL

1. Trim the zucchini and quarter them lengthwise. Cut them in half crosswise to form 1½- to 2-inch sticks.

2. Bring a large saucepan of salted water to a boil. Add half of the zucchini sticks and blanch for 30 seconds after the water returns to a boil. Remove with a slotted spoon and rinse under cold running water to stop the cooking. Repeat with the remaining zucchini.

3. Pack the zucchini, onion slices and dill sprigs into two 1-pint preserving jars. Bury 2 garlic cloves and 1 hot pepper in each.

4. In a small nonaluminum saucepan, combine the vinegar, sugar, salt and ¾ cup water. Slowly bring to a boil, stirring to dissolve the sugar. Pour the boiling liquid over the zucchini, dividing it evenly between the two jars. Let cool; then cover and refrigerate at least overnight before serving. These pickles improve markedly after 2 or 3 days and keep in the refrigerator for 3 to 4 weeks.

CHOCOLATE CHOCOLATE CHIP COOKIES

Like many, I cannot get enough chocolate. These cookies, inspired by my favorite ice cream, are made with both good-quality dark sweetened chocolate and cocoa powder.

Makes about 3 dozen

1 cup plus 2 tablespoons all-purpose flour
½ cup Dutch-process unsweetened cocoa
    powder
½ teaspoon baking powder
½ teaspoon baking soda
½ teaspoon salt
1 stick (4 ounces) unsalted butter, softened
1 cup sugar
1 egg
1 teaspoon vanilla
2 tablespoons sour cream
4½ ounces sweetened dark chocolate, such as
    Lindt Excellence or Tobler Extra Bitter-
    sweet, broken into bits

1. Preheat the oven to 350°F. Lightly butter 2 heavy cookie sheets.

2. Sift together the flour, cocoa, baking powder, baking soda and salt.

3. In a medium-size bowl, cream together the butter and sugar until light and fluffy. Beat in the egg and vanilla until smooth. Add the sour cream and mix until blended. Gradually stir in the dry ingredients until blended. Add the chocolate and fold to distribute evenly.

4. Drop the cookie dough by heaping teaspoons onto the prepared cookie sheets. Bake, reversing the sheets once to ensure even cooking, for 10 to 12 minutes. The shorter baking time will give you a softer, chewier cookie; the longer time, a crispier one. Transfer the cookies to racks and let them cool.

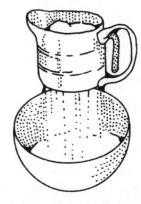

Little League Picnic

MENU

Serves 8–10

Deli-Style Chopped Chicken-Liver Spread*

Cocktail Rye Bread and/or Crackers

Assorted Cold Cuts: Pastrami, Corned Beef, Roast Beef, Turkey, Salami, Ham

Thinly Sliced Swiss Cheese, Tomatoes and Sweet Onions

Kosher Dill Pickles and Olives

Mayonnaise and Assortment of Mustards

Seeded Kaiser Rolls/Sliced Rye and Pumpernickel Breads

Creamy Coleslaw*

Quick Macaroni Salad*

Nectarines, Bananas and Plums

Marbled Sour Cream Coffeecake*

SPECIAL EQUIPMENT

Covered containers for chicken-liver spread, coleslaw and macaroni salad

Knives for spreading mayonnaise and mustard

Platter or board for cheese, tomatoes and onions

Bowls for condiments

Serving forks and spoons

Knife to cut cake

Large cooler to hold chicken-liver spread, cold cuts and cheese, mayonnaise, salads and beverages

This deli spread is for those times when you are feeding a large crowd and the food is secondary to the day's activities. It is perfectly suited for family picnics or outings with children, such as a day of Little League playoffs. Here the cook's most demanding chore is shopping.

My first choices for sandwich cold cuts are thinly sliced pastrami, corned beef, rare roast beef and turkey. Salami and baked ham are other possibilities. Allow a total of ⅓ to ½ pound meat per person, which should even cover seconds.

Let everyone choose their own combinations and make their own deli sandwiches. The selection of condiments will add to the festive feeling. Lay out sliced imported Swiss cheese, thinly sliced ripe tomatoes and sweet onions, olives, kosher dill pickles, mayonnaise and an assortment of mustards. Breads could include seeded kaiser rolls, split at home, and presliced rye and pumpernickel breads.

All the cook has to prepare is the chopped liver—a breeze in the food processor—and the Marbled Sour Cream Coffeecake, which can be made several days ahead. Kids love macaroni salad, which is quick and easy, as is Creamy Coleslaw, but both can be bought if you prefer. Substitute potato salad for the macaroni if you wish. The cake will provide 16 to 20 pieces. If there are more than ten people at the picnic, simply double the liver and salads.

For the adults, take along plenty of cold beer and iced tea or coffee; for the children, have a selection of fruit juices or punch.

DELI-STYLE CHOPPED CHICKEN-LIVER SPREAD

Traditionally this dish is made with rendered chicken fat, which is available in butcher shops and some supermarkets. I offer butter as an alternative that I find more easily digestible.

Makes about 2 cups

1 pound chicken livers, trimmed
4 tablespoons unsalted butter or rendered chicken fat
2 medium onions, chopped
1 teaspoon salt
½ teaspoon freshly ground black pepper
2 hard-cooked eggs, quartered
2 to 4 tablespoons chicken stock

1. Broil the chicken livers, turning once, until no longer pink.

2. In a large skillet, melt the butter over moderate heat. Add the onions and cook, stirring occasionally, until golden brown, about 10 minutes. Scrape the onions and butter into a food processor or blender.

3. Add the livers, salt and pepper; process by turning the machine on and off until the livers are coarsely chopped. Add the eggs and enough of the chicken stock to ensure a moist mixture and process until chopped.

CREAMY COLESLAW

Serves 8–10

½ cup sour cream
½ cup mayonnaise
1 tablespoon cider vinegar
1 tablespoon sugar
1 teaspoon dry mustard
½ teaspoon salt
¼ teaspoon freshly ground pepper
1 small head of cabbage (about 1 ½ pounds), shredded
2 medium carrots, shredded
2 scallions, chopped

1. In a large bowl, combine the sour cream, mayonnaise, vinegar, sugar, mustard, salt and pepper. Stir until blended.

2. Add the cabbage, carrots and scallions and toss until mixed.

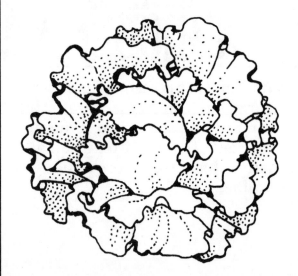

QUICK MACARONI SALAD

There is nothing fancy about this salad; it takes a total of 10 minutes to prepare. Kids love it, and so do a number of adults I know.

Serves 8–10

1 box (16 ounces) elbow macaroni
⅔ cup finely diced red bell pepper (about ½ large)
⅔ cup finely diced green bell pepper (about ½ large)
¼ cup finely diced onion (about 1 small)
1 cup mayonnaise
1 teaspoon sugar
1¼ teaspoons salt
¾ teaspoon freshly ground black pepper

1. In a large pot of boiling salted water, cook the macaroni until tender but still slightly firm, about 8 minutes. Drain and rinse under cold running water to stop the cooking; drain well.

2. In a large bowl, toss the cooled macaroni with the red pepper, green pepper and onion. Add the mayonnaise, sugar, salt and pepper and toss until well mixed. Refrigerate, covered, until serving time.

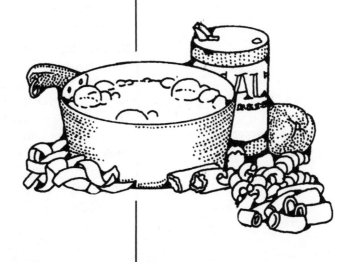

MARBLED SOUR CREAM COFFEECAKE

My mother gave me this recipe over a decade ago. Moist and dense, with swirls of tart vanilla and sweet chocolate, this cake is simple and irresistible. It keeps well and even improves after standing, tightly wrapped, overnight.

Serves 16

8 ounces dark sweetened chocolate
3 cups all-purpose flour
1½ teaspoons baking powder
1½ teaspoons baking soda
1 stick (4 ounces) butter, softened
1½ cups sugar
3 eggs
1 tablespoon vanilla
2 cups (1 pint) sour cream

1. Preheat the oven to 325°F. Grease a 10-inch tube pan. In the top of a double boiler, melt the chocolate over hot water. Remove from the heat and set aside.

2. Mix together the flour, baking powder and baking soda.

3. In a large bowl, cream the butter and sugar until light and fluffy. Beat in the eggs, one at a time, blending well after each addition. Beat in the vanilla and sour cream until blended. Gradually beat in the flour. The batter will be thick.

4. Stir approximately 1 cup of the vanilla batter into the melted chocolate. Spoon half of the remaining vanilla batter into the tube pan. Spoon a layer of half of the chocolate batter on top. Add a layer of the remaining vanilla batter and top with the remaining chocolate. Run a knife through the batter all around the pan, weaving back and forth to swirl the chocolate through the cake. Smooth the top with a rubber spatula to level, if necesssary.

5. Bake for 1 hour, or until the cake pulls away from the sides of the pan and a tester inserted in the center comes out clean, except perhaps for a little melted chocolate. Let stand for 5 minutes. Remove the outside of the pan. Let cool for 10 minutes. Then unmold and let cool before serving.

A Sunday Drive

When I was a child, Sundays often meant long drives in the country. Occasionally we would end up at an amusement park and sometimes at a relative's house, but more often than not the drives were aimless, winding through the green countryside, exploring shaded country lanes or scenic parks. Frequent as these outings were in fine weather, they always seemed to happen on the spur of the moment. Suddenly it was decided we would go, and my mother would toss together sandwiches, usually made of tuna fish, and bring along potato chips and whatever fresh fruit she could find in the refrigerator. The fact that it was a picnic made this simple lunch taste exquisite.

This menu provides a step up from sandwiches and plain fruit, yet its ease allows for the same last-minute getaway. The colorful and delicious tuna pasta salad can be tossed together literally in 15 to 20 minutes, depending on how long it takes the water to boil. Served at room temperature, it can sit in a picnic hamper or on a buffet table for several hours with no ill effect, and it keeps well in the refrigerator for up to two days.

TUNA PASTA SALAD WITH BROCCOLI AND SWEET PEPPER

If you follow the directions in the sequence below, you should be able to assemble this festive, colorful salad in 15 to 20 minutes. It is my favorite spur-of-the-moment salad, and it keeps well covered in the refrigerator for up to two days.

Serves 4

½ pound penne or rigatoni
1 bunch of broccoli (top only), divided into 1- to 1½-inch florets
1 medium carrot, peeled and cut into 1½-inch-long julienne strips
2 tablespoons red wine vinegar
¼ cup olive oil, preferably extra-virgin
1 medium red bell pepper, stemmed, seeded and cut into 1½-inch-long julienne strips
6 to 8 black brine-cured olives, pitted and slivered
2 large sun-dried tomatoes in olive oil, drained and cut crosswise into thin slices
1 can (7 ounces) tuna in olive oil, preferably Italian, drained and flaked
Salt and coarsely cracked black pepper

1. Bring a large pot of salted water to a boil for the pasta. Also bring a large saucepan of salted water to a boil. Cut up the vegetables.

2. In the large saucepan of boiling salted water, cook the broccoli for about 3 minutes, until tender and bright green but still slightly resistant to the bite. Remove with a large strainer or slotted spoon and rinse under cold running water to refresh; drain well. Transfer to a large bowl.

3. In the same boiling water, cook the carrot for about 1 minute, until just tender. Drain and add to the broccoli. Drizzle the vinegar and oil over the vegetables and toss; set aside to marinate.

4. When the pot of water is boiling, add the pasta and cook for 8 to 10 minutes, until tender but still slightly resistant to the bite; do not overcook. Drain in a colander and rinse under cold water until cool. Drain well, shaking the colander to remove water.

5. Add the pasta to the marinating vegetables. Add the red pepper, olives, sun-dried tomatoes and tuna. Toss to mix. Season lightly with salt and liberally with black pepper. Serve at room temperature.

Note If sun-dried tomatoes are not available, increase the number of olives to 10 or 12.

FRUIT SALAD WITH TOASTED COCONUT AND PECANS

The fruits listed below make a colorful presentation, but you can use almost any fruits you have on hand, including pineapple and melon.

Although the fruit salad is best assembled just before departing, it can macerate in the picnic hamper for several hours.

Serves 4–6

⅓ cup shredded coconut
⅓ cup coarsely chopped pecans
1 apple, cored and cubed
1 peach or nectarine, cubed
1 banana, thickly sliced
1 navel orange, peeled, sectioned and the sections halved
1 kiwi, peeled, halved lengthwise and sliced, or ¾ cup seedless green grapes
1 cup (½ pint) strawberries, raspberries or blackberries
½ cup orange juice, preferably fresh
2 tablespoons orange liqueur, such as Grand Marnier or Triple Sec
1 teaspoon lemon juice

1. Preheat the oven to 325°F. Spread out the coconut and pecans on a baking sheet and bake, tossing once or twice, for 10 to 15 minutes, until the coconut is lightly toasted. Turn out onto a plate and let cool.

2. Meanwhile, cut up all the fruits as directed in the ingredient list. In a large tightly lidded container, or in a serving bowl if you are making the salad for home use, combine the apple, peach, banana, orange, kiwi and berries. Add the orange juice, orange liqueur and lemon juice and toss to coat.

3. Let the fruit salad macerate at room temperature for at least an hour, tossing occasionally. If you are picnicking, carry the toasted coconut and pecans separately.

4. To serve, dish out the fruit salad, giving everyone some of the juices at the bottom. Top each serving with a spoonful or two of the coconut-pecan garnish. For home entertaining, sprinkle the toasted topping over the fruit salad in the serving bowl before bringing it to the table.

Marathon Party

MENU

Serves 4

Cold Spicy Noodles with
Peanut-Sesame Sauce*

Oriental Chicken Salad with Snow
Peas and Sweet Red Pepper*

Lychees and Loquats in Syrup

Almond Cookies

Lychee Tea and Fruit Juice

SPECIAL EQUIPMENT

Large covered containers for noodles
and chicken salad

Serving forks and spoon

Bowls for fruit

Forks or chopsticks

Cups for tea or juice

Thermos for tea and juice

Small cooler to hold chicken salad

Picnic hamper

Running has come into its own as a spectator sport in recent years. Marathons, especially, bring the crowds outdoors; and some all-day track meets have become traditional tailgate rallies. For such active picnics, when you might be running from one end of the park to the other to catch a glimpse of a good friend in competition, I try to bring a compact, easy-to-carry-and-serve picnic that has enough tempting taste and carbohydrate-loaded energy to satisfy the most ravenous appetites.

Here is a runner's favorite—pasta, in a more unusual guise—Chinese Cold Spicy Noodles with Peanut-Sesame Sauce. These are made with ordinary peanut butter and Chinese noodles, both available these days in the Chinese food section of most supermarkets. They are mouth-watering and taste just like the kind you get at restaurants. Fine made a day ahead, they can be transported and are best eaten at room temperature. The chicken salad, colorful with snow peas and sweet red pepper, is a good keeper too. For a few hours it will hold without any refrigeration, but to play it safe, if it is hot or if you plan to be out all day, carry it in a small cooler. A dessert of canned lychee nuts and loquats in their own syrup with store-bought almond cookies—Chinese, if you have access to an Oriental grocery—completes this simple but appealing menu. As a beverage, take a thermos of hot lychee tea and plenty of chilled fruit juices for the athletes.

COLD SPICY NOODLES WITH PEANUT-SESAME SAUCE

Many people are addicted to these hot spicy noodles. They are so tasty and need no special handling—perfect picnic fare. Serve slightly chilled or at room temperature. They keep well for several days.

In my supermarket, Chinese noodles are sold two slabs to a 10-ounce package; I use one here. If you buy fresh noodles, cook only until *al dente*.

Serves 4

5 ounces Chinese noodles
3½ tablespoons Oriental sesame oil
3 tablespoons peanut butter, at room temperature
1½ tablespoons soy sauce
1½ tablespoons rice wine vinegar
2 teaspoons sugar

¼ to ½ teaspoon Chinese hot oil, to taste (½ teaspoon is very hot)
1 tablespoon hot water
2 scallions, minced

1. In a large pot of boiling salted water, cook the noodles, gently separating the strands with a long fork or chopsticks as they soften, until barely tender, about 2 minutes. Drain and rinse under cold running water to stop the cooking; drain well. Dump into a bowl and toss with ½ tablespoon of the sesame oil to prevent sticking.

2. In a small bowl, gradually stir the remaining 3 tablespoons sesame oil into the peanut butter. Blend in the soy sauce, rice wine vinegar, sugar, hot oil and hot water. Spoon over the noodles. Toss to coat well.

3. Add the scallions and toss lightly. If you plan to hold the noodles overnight or longer, cover and refrigerate.

ORIENTAL CHICKEN SALAD WITH SNOW PEAS AND SWEET RED PEPPER

Here's another chicken salad, delicately seasoned with Oriental flavors.

Serves 4–6

1 ½ pounds chicken breasts, skinned and boned
¼ pound snow peas, ends trimmed and strings removed
3 tablespoons soy sauce
2 tablespoons Oriental sesame oil
1 tablespoon corn or peanut oil
1 tablespoon pale dry sherry or Shao Sing wine
½ teaspoon sugar
1 garlic clove, crushed through a press
1 teaspoon grated gingerroot
½ large red bell pepper, cut into strips 2 inches by ⅛ inch
2 or 3 scallions, split lengthwise and cut into 1-inch lengths
½ cup thinly sliced water chestnuts

1. In a large saucepan, simmer the chicken breasts in salted water to cover for about 20 minutes, until no longer pink in the center but still juicy. Remove from the water and let cool.

2. Meanwhile, blanch the snow peas in a pot of boiling water for about 30 seconds, until bright green but still crisp. Drain and rinse under cold running water; drain well.

3. In a small bowl, combine the soy sauce, sesame and corn oils, sherry and sugar. Stir to dissolve the sugar. Add the garlic and gingerroot to the dressing.

4. Cut the chicken into 1-inch squares. Pour on the soy dressing and toss to coat. Let the chicken marinate at room temperature for 30 minutes, or covered in the refrigerator for several hours, tossing occasionally.

5. Before serving, add the red pepper, scallions and water chestnuts. Toss to mix. Serve chilled or at room temperature.

A Country Outing

I first enjoyed this picnic many years ago under a grove of tall mango trees in Cuernavaca on a day's outing from Mexico City. The festivities were hosted by dear friends, the Valenzuelas, great cooks and lovers of good food.

The potato omelet is called a *frittata* in Spanish. Unlike a French-style omelet, it is cooked slowly over low heat, producing a thick, firm texture, easy to wrap and transport, and even sturdy enough to pick up in your hands to eat. It keeps beautifully in the refrigerator overnight. Pistou is a Spanish version of ratatouille, without any eggplant. Zesty and light, it makes a perfect accompaniment to the eggs.

These are recipes that are simple and can be prepared a day in advance, in the case of the omelet, or a good two days ahead, in the case of the Pistou. This menu is appropriate for almost any season, best at room temperature and easy to serve and eat. In short, it is perfect tailgate fare.

SPANISH POTATO OMELET

Serves 4

¼ cup olive oil
1 pound red potatoes (3 large), peeled and
    cut into ⅛-inch-thick slices
1 medium onion, cut into ⅜-inch dice
7 eggs, lightly beaten
Salt and freshly ground black pepper
Dash of Tabasco sauce

1. In a 10-inch ovenproof skillet, heat 3 table-spoons of the oil. Add the potato slices and cook over moderately high heat, turning frequently, until they begin to brown on both sides, about 10 minutes.

2. Add the onion and season liberally with salt and pepper. Reduce the heat to moderately low. Cook, turning frequently, for 5 minutes. Cover the skillet and cook, turning once or twice, until the potatoes are browned outside and tender inside and the onions are soft and beginning to brown, about 5 minutes longer.

3. Uncover the skillet, add the remaining 1 tablespoon oil and let heat for about 15 seconds. Meanwhile, beat the eggs lightly with ¼ teaspoon salt, ⅛ teaspoon pepper and the Tabasco sauce. Pour over the potatoes and cook, covered, over moderately low heat until the frittata is firm around the edges, about 5 minutes; the center will still be soft.

4. Slip the frittata out of the skillet onto a platter or plate and carefully invert back into the pan. Cook uncovered until the egg is set throughout, about 3 minutes. Serve hot or at room temperature, cut into wedges like a pie.

PISTOU

Serves 6–8

¼ cup olive oil
2 medium onions, chopped
2 pounds zucchini, cut into ⅜-inch dice
½ pound bell peppers, preferably 1 green
    and 1 red, cut into ¼-inch dice
1 tablespoon finely chopped garlic
½ pound ripe tomatoes, peeled, seeded and
    chopped
1 teaspoon salt
½ teaspoon freshly ground black pepper
Several dashes of cayenne pepper
1 tablespoon fresh lemon juice
1 tablespoon red wine vinegar

1. In a large flameproof casserole, heat the oil over moderate heat. Add the onions and sauté until they soften and begin to color, 5 to 10 minutes.

2. Add the zucchini, bell peppers and garlic. Increase the heat to moderately high and cook, stirring frequently, for 5 minutes.

3. Add the tomatoes, salt, black pepper and cayenne. Cook until the zucchini and bell peppers are tender but still hold their shape, 3 to 5 minutes longer.

4. Remove from the heat and toss with the lemon juice and vinegar. Serve warm, at room temperature or chilled.

At the Ballpark

MENU

Serves 4–6

Roasted Peanuts

Pita Pocket Sandwiches Filled with Tuna, Chicken, Ham or Egg Salad

Garnishes for Sandwiches: Shredded Romaine Lettuce, Sliced Olives, Coarsely Chopped Tomatoes, Shredded Swiss, Cheddar or Monterey Jack Cheese

Confetti Corn Salad*

Walnut-Rum Squares with Chocolate Icing*

Cold Soda or Beer

SPECIAL EQUIPMENT

Covered container for corn salad

Small covered containers for garnishes

Spoons for serving garnishes

Serving spoon for salad

Small cooler for filled sandwiches and shredded cheese

What's a baseball game without hot roasted peanuts, the shells crunching underneath your shoes, and huge paper cups of beer? Nibbles in the bleachers are great, but when it comes to real food, you're in trouble, unless you're a fan of shriveled hot dogs in soggy buns. That's why I like to take a picnic to the game.

Pita bread makes the perfect holder for sandwich fillings. Simply slice through one layer of the bread near the top, fill it halfway with tuna, chicken, ham or egg salad and top with a choice of tasty garnishes. Confetti Corn Salad, a dry relish, is a colorful accompaniment, though it does necessitate paper plates and forks.

Carry the sandwiches in a small cooler. Buy soda or beer at the stadium. The corn salad is best served at room temperature, as are the Walnut-Rum Squares, though the frosting will soften on a very hot day.

CONFETTI CORN SALAD

Serves 4–6

3 tablespoons corn oil
1 large onion, diced
½ large green pepper, cut into ¼-inch dice
  (about ½ cup)
½ large red pepper, cut into ¼-inch dice
  (about ½ cup)
1 large garlic clove, minced
3 cups corn kernels (3 to 4 large ears of corn,
  or two 11-ounce cans)
1 teaspoon salt
½ teaspoon ground cumin
⅛ to ¼ teaspoon crushed hot red pepper, to
  taste
1½ tablespoons fresh lime juice

1. In a large skillet, heat the oil. Add the onion and sauté over moderately high heat, stirring occasionally, until lightly browned, 5 to 7 minutes. Add the green and red peppers and the garlic and cook until the peppers are slightly softened but still crisp, about 2 minutes.

2. Add the corn, salt, cumin and hot pepper. Reduce the heat to moderate and cook, tossing, until the corn is tender but still firm, about 5 minutes. Remove from the heat, sprinkle on the lime juice and toss. Serve hot, at room temperature or chilled.

WALNUT-RUM SQUARES WITH CHOCOLATE ICING

This is a low cake, in the classic European nut-torte fashion. It contains only ¼ cup flour. I derived this recipe from a marvelous almond cake, Pain de Gênes, taught to me by Richard Grausman of the Cordon Bleu. It takes literally just a few minutes to prepare in the food processor.

Serves 6–8

Butter and flour for baking pan
1 can (3 ounces) walnuts
½ cup sugar
¼ cup all-purpose flour
Pinch of salt
1 stick (4 ounces) unsalted butter
3 eggs
2 tablespoons dark or amber rum
1 teaspoon vanilla

Chocolate Icing

Makes about ½ cup
4 ounces bittersweet or semisweet chocolate
2 tablespoons coffee or dark rum
2 tablespoons unsalted butter, cut into pieces

1. Preheat the oven to 350°F. Butter an 8-inch-square cake pan. Line the bottom with waxed paper. Butter and flour the paper and the sides of the pan.

2. In a food processor, grind the walnuts with ¼ cup of the sugar, turning the machine on and off twice and then letting it run for about 20 seconds to produce a fine grind. Add the flour and salt and turn on and off once to blend. Turn into a bowl. (There is no need to rinse the machine at this point.)

3. Add the butter and remaining ¼ cup sugar to the processor. Beat until smooth, scraping down the sides of the bowl as necessary. Add the eggs, one at a time, mixing well for about 5 seconds after each addition. Add the rum and vanilla and blend. Add the nut-flour mixture and mix briefly until just blended.

4. Pour the batter into the prepared cake pan. Tap lightly to settle. Bake in the middle of the oven for 35 to 40 minutes, until the top is golden and the edges are beginning to pull away from the side of the pan.

5. Invert the cake onto a rack. Peel off the waxed paper and let the cake cool.

6. To make the icing, melt the chocolate in the coffee or rum in a small heavy saucepan, over low heat, stirring until smooth.

7. Remove from the heat and stir in the butter until blended and smooth. Frost the top of the cake with Chocolate Icing and cut into 2-inch squares.

GRILLING OUT

The Fourth of July

SPECIAL EQUIPMENT

Wide-mouth thermos for soup

Soup bowls or mugs

Portable grill

Charcoal and matches

Asbestos mitts

Long-handled tongs and two-prong
fork

Platter for chicken

Serving pieces for chicken, salads
and pie

Knife for cornbread

Thermos for coffee

The birthday of this country's independence occasions many all-day outings. Whether your plans include a day at the beach, a picnic in a state park or a group of friends gathering for the local fireworks, you'll want to be sure to have plenty of food on hand. This menu celebrates America's bounty with traditional ingredients like sweet corn and blueberries, reminding us of the wealth our land has to offer.

Start with savory Ham and Cheese Stuffed Eggs, complete with mustard and pickles. They can be pulled out of the cooler as an afternoon snack, or served as an early appetizer while the grill is heating up to cook the chicken. Corn-Tomato Chowder is one of my favorite soups. Made from native butter-and-sugar corn and vine-ripened tomatoes, it has a fresh appeal and natural sweetness that reminds us why it is well worth a visit to the local farmer's market. In winter, the soup can be made with canned or frozen corn and canned tomatoes, but the flavor will not be quite the same.

Barbecued chicken is always popular, and this is an excellent recipe for it. Marinate the chicken in the cooler all day. Remove the chicken from the cooler and light the grill about 45 minutes to 1 hour before you plan to start cooking. Creamy Old-Fashioned Potato Salad and tart sliced cucumbers in vinegar provide a nice counterpoint of textures and flavors to serve alongside. Pass biscuits or cornbread (see page 121) as an accompaniment. Drink lemonade or cold beer. As an apéritif, you might like to try a Nantucket cocktail: 3 parts cranberry juice and 1 part vodka.

For dessert, an old-fashioned dessert, Blueberry Pie, flavored with a splash of Grand Marnier, and a bowl of Bing cherries, for a patriotic red, white and blue finale.

HAM AND CHEESE STUFFED EGGS

Serves 6

6 hard-cooked eggs
¼ cup mayonnaise
1 tablespoon Dijon-style mustard
⅛ teaspoon salt
¼ teaspoon freshly ground pepper
Several dashes of Tabasco sauce, to taste
2 teaspoons minced fresh dill, or ¼ teaspoon dried dillweed (optional)
2 ounces ham, preferably baked, cut into ¼-inch dice
2 ounces Swiss cheese, cut into ⅛-inch dice

1 ½ tablespoons minced sweet gherkin pickles

1. Halve the eggs lengthwise. Remove the yolks; set the whites aside.

2. In a small bowl, mash the egg yolks. Add the mayonnaise, mustard, salt, pepper, Tabasco sauce and dill, if you like it; blend to a paste. Add the ham, cheese and pickle and stir to mix.

3. Mound the filling in the egg whites. Cover and refrigerate until serving time.

CORN-TOMATO CHOWDER

Serves 6

¼ pound slab bacon, cut into ¼-inch dice
3 tablespoons unsalted butter
2 large onions, cut into ⅜-inch dice
2 tablespoons all-purpose flour
2 large ripe tomatoes, peeled, seeded and
    coarsely chopped
1 quart milk
1 teaspoon salt
¼ teaspoon freshly ground pepper
¼ teaspoon crumbled sage
⅛ teaspoon grated nutmeg
1 small bay leaf
2 medium red potatoes, peeled and cut into
    ⅜-inch dice
2 cups corn kernels (from 2 to 3 ears of corn)
¾ teaspoon fresh lemon juice
Dash of cayenne pepper

1. Blanch the bacon in a saucepan of boiling water for 5 minutes. Drain and rinse briefly; drain well. Pat dry on paper towels.

2. In a large flameproof casserole, melt the butter over moderate heat. Add the onions and cook, stirring occasionally, until softened and translucent, about 5 minutes.

3. Add the bacon and cook, stirring frequently, until the onions are golden, about 5 minutes. Sprinkle on the flour and cook, stirring, for about 2 minutes without letting the flour color. Add the tomatoes. If they are very juicy, cook, stirring, until most of the moisture evaporates, 2 to 3 minutes.

4. Gradually whisk in the milk. Season with the salt, pepper, sage, nutmeg and bay leaf. Bring to a boil and add the potatoes. Reduce the heat and simmer, partially covered, stirring occasionally, for 10 minutes.

5. Add the corn and continue to simmer, partially covered, until the corn and potatoes are tender, about 10 minutes longer. Add the lemon juice and cayenne. Season with additional salt and pepper to taste. Serve hot.

BARBECUED CHICKEN

I like to marinate the chickens in the barbecue sauce so they pick up as much flavor as possible. If you do this, pack them with the sauce in plastic containers with tight-fitting lids either the night before or the day of the picnic. Carry in a cooler, but remove 30 minutes to 1 hour before grilling to allow the chicken to warm up slightly before cooking.

Serves 6–8

2 chickens (about 3 pounds each), cut into 8
    serving pieces
¾ cup ketchup
½ cup cider vinegar

½ cup brown sugar
3 tablespoons Worcestershire sauce
3 tablespoons vegetable oil
2 tablespoons fresh lemon juice
2 tablespoons chili powder
2 teaspoons Dijon-style mustard
¼ teaspoon Tabasco sauce, or to taste
1 teaspoon salt
½ teaspoon freshly ground black pepper
1 small onion, minced
2 garlic cloves, minced

1. Mix all the sauce ingredients together and marinate the chicken overnight in the refrigerator, or several hours in the cooler.

2. Grill the chicken, turning once or twice and basting repeatedly with the marinade, until done, 15 to 20 minutes.

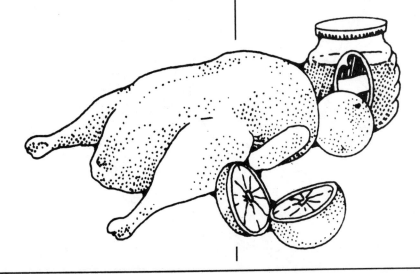

OLD-FASHIONED POTATO SALAD

Serves 6

6 medium red or other waxy potatoes (1 ½ or
    2 pounds)
½ cup mayonnaise
¼ cup sour cream
1 ½ tablespoons red wine vinegar
1 teaspoon Dijon-style mustard
½ teaspoon salt
¼ teaspoon freshly ground pepper
1 medium celery rib, chopped
1 small onion, finely chopped
1 hard-cooked egg, coarsely chopped

1. In a large saucepan of boiling water, cook the potatoes until tender, about 25 minutes.

2. Drain into a colander, rinse briefly under cold water and let drain for at least 10 minutes until cool enough to handle. Then peel off the skins and thickly slice the potatoes or cut into chunks if you prefer.

3. In a large bowl, combine the mayonnaise, sour cream, vinegar, mustard, salt and pepper. Stir to blend the dressing.

4. Add the celery, onion and potatoes and fold until the vegetables are mixed and coated with dressing. Add the egg and blend lightly.

5. Cover and refrigerate or chill in a cooler until serving time.

BLUEBERRY PIE

Makes one 9-inch pie with lattice top

Butter Crust Pastry

2 ½ cups all-purpose flour
1 ½ tablespoons sugar
1 teaspoon salt
1 ½ sticks (6 ounces) unsalted butter, chilled
  and cut into small bits
3 to 4 tablespoons ice water

Filling

2 pints (4 cups) blueberries
2 ½ tablespoons cornstarch
3 tablespoons orange liqueur, such as Triple
  Sec or Grand Marnier
1 tablespoon lemon juice
½ teaspoon cinnamon
½ to ¾ cup sugar
2 tablespoons unsalted butter

1. Make the pastry: In a medium-size bowl, combine the flour, sugar and salt. Cut in the butter until the mixture resembles coarse meal. Gradually drizzle in the ice water while tossing with a fork until the dough begins to mass together.

2. Turn out onto a lightly floured surface, and quickly smear small amounts of the dough away from you with the heel of your hand to blend further. Gather into a ball, wrap in wax paper and a plastic bag and re-frigerate for at least 30 minutes before rolling out.

3. Make the filling: Rinse the berries and drain well. Pick them over to remove any green berries or twigs.

4. In a medium-size bowl, stir together the cornstarch, orange liqueur, lemon juice and cinnamon until blended. Add the berries and ½ cup sugar and toss to coat. Let stand, tossing occasionally, for about 20 minutes. Taste and add additional sugar if desired.

5. Preheat the oven to 425°F. Roll out two-thirds of the pastry into a round about ⅛ inch thick. Fit the pastry into a 9-inch pie pan. Trim the edges to allow a ½-inch over-hang. Fold over the excess; press and crimp to make a raised scalloped edge.

6. Pour the blueberry filling into the piecrust. Dot with the butter.

7. Roll out the remaining pastry about ⅛ inch thick. Cut into ½- to ¾-inch strips and form into a lattice top.

8. Bake the pie in the middle of the oven for 15 minutes. Reduce the heat to 350°F. and bake for about 45 minutes longer, until the filling is syrupy and bubbling and the crust is golden brown.

Patio Party

MENU

Serves 6

Taramasalata*

Babaganoush*

Toasted Pita Triangles

Shish Kebab*

Tabbouleh*

Pita Bread

Greek Salad

Kalamata Olives

Baklava

Greek Coffee and Ouzo

SPECIAL EQUIPMENT

Covered containers for transporting the Taramasalata, Babaganoush, Tabbouleh, Greek salad and marinating meat

Serving dishes and spoons

Salad bowl and servers for Greek salad

Basket for pita triangles and bread

Bowl for olives

Long metal skewers and platter for shish kebab

Portable grill

Charcoal and matches

Asbestos mitts

Wineglasses

Cups

Thermos for coffee

Large cooler for transporting Taramasalata, marinating meat and wine

This Greek menu is marvelous for any picnic or outdoor party. Except for the Tabbouleh—a whole-grain wheat salad with lots of chopped parsley, mint, tomato and onion, tart with lemon—this entire meal can be consumed with no silverware whatsoever. Toasted triangles of pita bread can be used as scoops for the Taramasalata and Babaganoush. Serve the Shish Kebab in whole pita breads, like souvlaki. If you prefer more formal service, the grilled meat and vegetables can be served on plates, with the Tabbouleh as a side dish and the pita as a bread accompaniment.

This is tasty, festive food, appropriate for partying. The Taramasalata, a fish roe spread, and the uncooked meat should be kept in a cooler. The other dishes can be transported at room temperature. Good-quality leg of lamb, cooked rare to medium rare, will ensure a tender Shish Kebab. If you end up with a large crowd and want to add another dish, throw together a big Greek salad—romaine lettuce, chunks of ripe tomato, green bell pepper, purple onion, cucumber, red pepper, anchovies and feta cheese, tossed in a vinaigrette with a little oregano. Put out plenty of good Kalamata olives and pita bread.

Have on hand a large supply of slightly chilled, easy-drinking Greek red wine. After the dessert of store-bought Baklava, pull out a thermos of Greek coffee or espresso and pass around a bottle of iced Ouzo for extra good cheer.

TARAMASALATA

Makes about 1½ cups

2 slices of firm-textured white bread, crusts removed
⅓ cup tarama (carp roe, available in the refrigerated sections of Greek groceries and specialty food shops)
1 tablespoon coarsely chopped onion
1 garlic clove, crushed through a press
¼ cup fresh lemon juice
⅔ cup olive oil

1. In a shallow dish, soak the bread slices in water to cover until soft and pasty. Squeeze with your hands to remove as much water as possible.

2. In a blender or food processor, combine the bread paste, tarama, onion, garlic and lemon juice. Process until blended.

3. With the machine on, gradually pour in the oil. Serve with pita bread and Kalamata olives.

BABAGANOUSH

This tasty vegetable purée can be served as a dip for *crudités* or pieces of pita bread or as a salad. I make it with only 1 tablespoon of oil; the creaminess of the eggplant, though low in calories, makes it taste rich enough.

Makes about 3 cups

2 medium eggplants (about 1 pound each)
2 tablespoons tahini (sesame paste)
⅓ cup fresh lemon juice
1 tablespoon olive oil
1 large garlic clove, crushed through a press
½ teaspoon salt
6 parsley sprigs

1. Pierce the eggplants once or twice with a fork. Broil them as close to the source of heat as possible, turning, until charred all over, about 20 minutes.

2. As soon as the eggplants can be handled, cut off and discard the green tops and remove the skin. Also discard any large clumps of seeds. Put the eggplant in a food processor or blender and purée.

3. Add the tahini, lemon juice, olive oil, garlic and salt and process until blended. Add the parsley and process until it is minced. Taste and adjust the seasonings if necessary. Serve at room temperature or slightly chilled.

SHISH KEBAB

If packing these up for a picnic, prepare through Step 2. Wrap up the kebabs already assembled and transport in a cooler.

Serves 6

2 pounds boneless leg of lamb, cut into 1½-inch cubes
¾ cup dry red wine

¼ cup olive oil, preferably extra-virgin
2 garlic cloves, crushed through a press
½ teaspoon oregano
¼ teaspoon thyme
1 bay leaf
Salt and freshly ground pepper
1 large onion, cut into 1-inch squares
1 large green bell pepper, cut into 1-inch squares
12 cherry tomatoes
12 medium mushrooms, stemmed

1. Trim off any excess fat from the lamb. In a large bowl, combine the wine, oil, garlic, oregano, thyme and bay leaf. Add the lamb and marinate at room temperature, tossing occasionally, for 1 to 2 hours, or in the refrigerator overnight.

2. Remove the meat from the marinade and pat dry with paper towels. Season liberally with salt and pepper. Thread the meat on 6 long metal skewers, alternating the cubes of lamb with the pieces of onion and green pepper, the tomatoes and mushroom caps.

3. Grill over a hot fire or broil, turning, until the lamb is cooked to desired doneness, 5 to 10 minutes.

TABBOULEH

Serves 6

1 cup bulgur or cracked wheat
½ cup olive oil
⅓ cup fresh lemon juice
1 cup chopped parsley
½ cup chopped mint
½ cup chopped scallions
2 medium tomatoes, seeded and chopped
1 teaspoon salt
½ teaspoon freshly ground pepper

1. Place the bulgur in a medium bowl and add cold water to cover by 2 inches. Let stand until softened but still slightly resistant to the bite, about 1 hour.

2. Drain well; place the bulgur in a clean towel and squeeze out as much excess water as possible.

3. In a bowl, combine the bulgur with the oil, lemon juice, parsley, mint, scallions, tomatoes, salt and pepper. Toss to blend well. Serve at room temperature or slightly chilled.

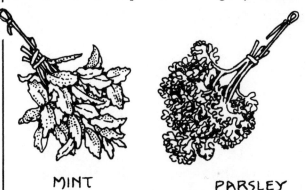

MINT   PARSLEY

At the Beach

MENU

Serves 4–6

Grilled Clams with Garlic Butter

Skewered Swordfish, Shrimp and Scallops*

Roasted Corn

Chunky Vegetable Salad with Sour Cream Dressing*

Semolina Bread

Watermelon Filled with Fruit Salad

Chocolate Chocolate Chip Cookies (see page 59)

SPECIAL EQUIPMENT

Portable grill

Charcoal and matches

Asbestos mitts

Long metal skewers

Covered containers for seafood, vegetable salad and fruit salad

Cooler for clams, kebabs and salads

Just thinking about the heat of an August sun, the smell of suntan lotion and the salt of the sea makes me hungry. Maybe that's because since I'm always ravenous after a day at the beach, I always try to take along a fabulous tailgate feast. This is one of my favorites, redolent with the flavors of the ocean. In fact, whenever possible, I prepare the marinade for the Skewered Swordfish, Shrimp and Scallops at home and buy the seafood, along with the clams for grilling, at a fish market along the shore. The market cuts up the fish for me, and the seafood has plenty of time to marinate in an ice chest while we're lying on the sand. I also like to buy the corn at a roadside stand on the way so it will be fresh and sweet.

The garlic butter for the clams should be prepared at home and later reheated in a small saucepan on the grill. To make the garlic butter, steep 2 to 3 crushed garlic cloves in 1 stick (4 ounces) of melted unsalted butter for a few minutes. Vegetables for the salad and the sour cream dressing are also prepared at home and tossed together before serving. The fruit salad can be made with any combination of fruits and berries in season that you have on hand. If watermelon is one of them, use the scooped-out shell as a striking serving piece.

Light the grill 45 minutes to 1 hour before you plan to eat. Grill the clams over the hot coals, covered if possible, just until they open. Either littlenecks or cherrystones work beautifully this way. While they are cooking, warm the garlic butter on the edge of the grill. Have plenty of lemon wedges on hand for both the clams and seafood kebabs, and a chest full of ice-cold beer.

SKEWERED SWORDFISH, SHRIMP AND SCALLOPS

Serves 4

1 pound swordfish steak, cut 1 inch thick, skin removed, meat cut into 1-inch chunks
½ pound medium to large shrimp, shelled and deveined
½ pound sea scallops
3 tablespoons olive oil, preferably virgin
3 tablespoons fresh lemon juice
6 bay leaves, broken in half
3 garlic cloves, crushed
Salt and freshly ground pepper
Lemon wedges

1. In a large bowl, combine the swordfish, shrimp and scallops. Add the olive oil, lemon juice, bay leaves and garlic. Toss to mix. Let marinate at room temperature, tossing occasionally, for 1 to 2 hours, or cover and place in the refrigerator or a cooler for up to 8 hours.

2. Light the charcoal or preheat the broiler. Thread the seafood onto 4 long metal skewers, alternating the ingredients and placing a bay leaf half next to the swordfish. Season liberally with salt and pepper.

3. Grill over hot coals, about 3 inches from the heat, turning, until the swordfish is just cooked through, 5 to 6 minutes. Serve with plenty of lemon wedges. (Do not eat the bay leaves.)

CHUNKY VEGETABLE SALAD WITH SOUR CREAM DRESSING

Serves 4–6

1 large ripe tomato, cut into ⅜-inch dice
1 large cucumber, peeled, seeded and cut
　　into ⅜-inch dice
6 radishes, cut into ⅜-inch dice
1 medium green bell pepper, cut into ⅜-inch
　　squares
2 scallions, sliced
½ cup sour cream
1 tablespoon white wine vinegar
1 teaspoon sugar
½ teaspoon salt
¼ teaspoon freshly ground pepper
2 tablespoons chopped fresh parsley
1 tablespoon chopped fresh dill (optional)
1 tablespoon chopped fresh mint (optional)

1. Prepare all the vegetables and toss them together in a serving bowl or lidded container.

2. In a small bowl or container, stir together the sour cream, vinegar, sugar, salt, pepper, parsley and dill and/or mint if you have them, to make the dressing. If not serving shortly, cover the vegetables and dressing separately and refrigerate or transport in a cooler or ice chest.

3. Shortly before serving, add the sour cream dressing to the vegetables and toss until coated.

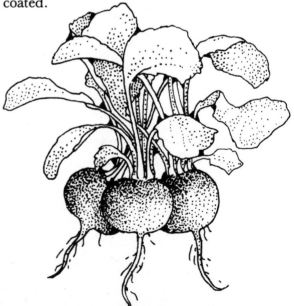

Viewing the Cherry Blossoms

Menu

Serves 6

Marinated Goat Cheese in Olive Oil
with Herbs*

Crackers

Green Bean Salad Provençale*

Herb-Grilled Lamb Steaks*

Tabbouleh (see page 87)
or French-Style Potato Salad
(see page 112)

Quick Strawberry Shortcake (see
page 49) or Fresh Fruit

Special Equipment

Covered container, plate and
spreader for goat cheese

Basket for crackers

Portable grill

Charcoal and matches

Asbestos mitt

Long-handled fork

Covered containers for transporting
lamb, bean salad and tabbouleh

Domed cake platter

Salad servers and serving spoon

Cake knife

Cooler for cheese, lamb and
strawberry shortcake

In Japan, the Cherry Blossom Festival is celebrated every year on April 8. Miraculously, nature somehow cooperates, and the magnificent trees bloom on that date. The cherry trees in this country are not as predictable, and the best times to view the blossoms vary from state to state, but whenever it does occur, it is one of spring's treats, one well worth sharing with good friends or family. Here is a charming menu, worthy of the occasion and featuring some of spring's finest foods.

Though we produce excellent lamb all year round, it is traditionally mildest in the spring. I'm partial to grilled butterflied leg of lamb, but it takes a good-size grill and some time to cook, not always practical for a tailgate. I've found that lamb steaks cut from the shank part of the leg make a fine substitute. This is very dense, lean meat and should be seared quickly to rare or medium-rare only, to remain tender and juicy. I add extra flavor by marinating the lamb first in fruity olive oil, fresh lemon juice, fragrant herbs and garlic. The same treatment works beautifully for lamb chops. If you have an extra handful of dry herbs, throw them on the grill just before you add the lamb.

Beans are the classic accompaniment to lamb, and a bright salad of green beans, sweet onions and Niçoise olives is perfect here. Zesty tabbouleh, full of fresh parsley and mint, makes a pleasant side dish, but you can serve a potato salad if you prefer.

Begin with herbed goat cheese marinated in olive oil, which can be made days in advance as long as the cheese is kept covered with oil. Refrigerate for longer storage, but leave out at room temperature long enough for the oil to melt, if it has congealed. For picnicking, it is easiest to remove the cheeses from the oil before you set out. They will continue to exude oil, so be sure to carry them in a tightly sealed container. Save the oil for salad dressing; it is full of flavor!

April is also the start of strawberry season and a fine time to complete your meal with the Quick Strawberry Shortcake on page 49. You might enjoy them plain, with a bowl of sugar for dipping, for a lighter finale.

MARINATED GOAT CHEESE IN OLIVE OIL WITH HERBS

These tasty little cylinders of cheese are now available in most cheese shops, but they are quite expensive. They are simple to prepare at home, at a fraction of the cost. Use the leftover oil from marinating the cheese on ripe tomatoes or on leafy salads.

Serves 6–8

1 log (8 ounces) Montrachet blanc (Other mild goat cheese can be used, though the shape of Montrachet is ideal for this recipe.)
About 1 teaspoon *herbes de Provence*
Freshly ground black pepper
2 garlic cloves, smashed
1 small dried hot red pepper
Extra-virgin olive oil

1. Cut the log of cheese into quarters. Sprinkle each end of the 4 small cylinders with about ⅛ teaspoon of *herbes de Provence*. Season with pepper. Pat the seasonings lightly so they adhere to the cheese.

2. Arrange the cheese cylinders in a container just large enough to hold them, either stacked or in a single layer. Add the garlic and red pepper. Pour in enough olive oil to cover. Let marinate at room temperature for at least 3 hours before serving. If the oil congeals after being refrigerated, simply let stand at room temperature until it melts.

GREEN BEAN SALAD PROVENÇALE

Follow directions for Green Bean and Shrimp Salad Provençale (page 113), but:

1. Omit the shrimp.

2. Increase the green beans to 1¼ pounds.

3. In Step 4, add ¼ cup Niçoise olives and 2 ripe tomatoes, peeled, seeded and cut into strips.

HERB-GRILLED LAMB STEAKS

Serves 6

4 lamb steaks, cut about ¾ inch thick from the shank of the leg (2½ to 3 pounds total), or use an equivalent amount of lamb chops
4 garlic cloves, crushed
½ cup olive oil, preferably extra-virgin
2 teaspoons *herbes de Provence*
8 to 12 sprigs of parsley
8 to 12 sprigs of fresh thyme, or 2 teaspoons dried
8 to 12 sprigs of fresh oregano, or 1 teaspoon dried
3 tablespoons fresh lemon juice
Salt and freshly ground pepper

1. Trim off any excess fat from the sides of the lamb. Score the outside edge of the steaks, cutting just through the filament at intervals, so the lamb doesn't curl when it is grilled.

2. Rub the garlic and oil into both sides of the meat. Sprinkle about ¼ teaspoon of *herbes de Provence* onto both sides of each steak. In a baking dish large enough to hold the lamb in a single layer, arrange half of the fresh herbs, bruising them with your fingers to bring out their volatile oils. Lay the lamb steaks on top. Press the remaining herbs into the lamb and sprinkle on the lemon juice. Let marinate at room temperature for several hours, or in the refrigerator or a cooler for longer, turning oc-casionally. (If the lamb has been chilled, let return to room temperature before cooking.)

3. Light the charcoal or preheat the broiler. Scrape the herbs and garlic off the lamb. Season both sides of the steaks with salt and pepper. Grill over hot coals, about 3 inches from the heat, turning once, until rare, 4 to 5 minutes, or a minute longer for medium rare.

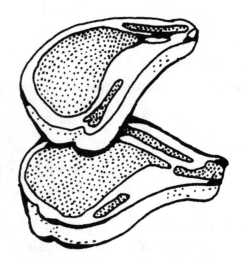

94

Memorial Day Tailgate

Menu

Serves 6

Pickled Shrimp*

Cheddar Cheese and Crackers

Grilled Marinated Flank Steak*

Grilled Eggplant and Zucchini
Slices*

Cauliflower Salad with Sun-Dried
Tomatoes*

Crusty French Bread

Peach Turnovers*

Special Equipment

Covered containers for shrimp, steak
and cauliflower salad

Bowl and toothpicks for shrimp

Cheeseboard and knife

Portable grill

Charcoal and matches

Long-handled fork

Basting brush

Serving bowl and spoon for
cauliflower salad

Cutting board and knife to slice
steak

Cooler for shrimp, cheese and steak

Thermos for beverage

For many, Memorial Day signals the first warm-weather outing of the year. In my hometown, we called it "beach weekend" and made an annual pilgrimage to the shore, though given the vagrancy of late-May weather, bathing suits often ended up swathed over with sweaters and blankets, and by dusk we welcomed the heat from the warm coals of the grill.

This menu is perfectly suited to both the sunny skies and brisk winds of this pivotal season. And in keeping with the activity-oriented spirit of the holiday, it is an easy picnic to put together and serve.

The zesty Pickled Shrimp can be made weeks in advance. Drain off the marinade before leaving the house and carry the shrimp in a tightly sealed container in a cooler or ice chest. Bring along plenty of toothpicks to spear them with and cocktail napkins to catch oily drips. Cheddar cheese can be chunked or sliced at home for convenience and tightly wrapped or carried whole, in which case bring a small cheeseboard and knife. Marinate the flank steak the night before, or just before you leave the house. Use a shallow, tightly lidded plastic container large enough for the steak to lie flat. Keep it in the cooler during the day, but bring the meat to room temperature before grilling. Slice the eggplant and zucchini at home and salt the pieces lightly with coarse salt to draw out the moisture. Wrap in paper towels in a plastic bag and bring extra paper towels to pat the slices dry before cooking.

The peach turnovers will keep if made the day before, though I prefer them freshly baked. Even though they can be picked up and eaten by hand, they are fragile; pack them cushioned with some crumpled plastic wrap in a hard covered container to protect them from being crushed.

PICKLED SHRIMP

Makes 1 quart, enough for 6–8 appetizer servings

1 pound medium shrimp, in their shells
1 small lemon
1 small onion, thinly sliced
6 sprigs of parsley
1 garlic clove, split lengthwise in half
1 dried hot red pepper
1 bay leaf
1¼ cups cider vinegar
3 tablespoons olive oil
1½ tablespoons mixed pickling spice
1 teaspoon sugar
1 teaspoon salt
½ teaspoon dry mustard

1. Peel and devein the shrimp, leaving the tails attached. Bring a large pot of salted water to the boil. Add the shrimp and cook until they are pink and just curled, about 1 minute after the water returns to the boil. Drain.

2. With a sharp stainless-steel knife, cut the peel with all the white pith off the lemon. Cut the lemon pulp into thin slices.

3. Put the shrimp in a 1-quart Mason jar, alternating them with slices of onion and lemon and interspersing with sprigs of parsley. Tuck the garlic pieces, hot pepper and bay leaf into the jar.

4. In a medium-size nonaluminum saucepan, combine the vinegar, oil, pickling spice, sugar, salt and mustard. Add ¾ cup water and bring to a boil over moderate heat, stirring to dissolve the sugar. Pour the hot mixture over the shrimp. Let stand until cooled; then cover and refrigerate at least overnight and for up to 3 weeks before serving.

GRILLED MARINATED FLANK STEAK

This steak is markedly superior when served rare. Increase the cooking time if you prefer it more well done. If you happen to grow or have some fresh herbs on hand, bring along a handful—rosemary, thyme, marjoram—and throw them on top of the hot coals just before you grill the steak. For a picnic add the beef to the marinade in the morning and transport it in a tightly covered container in a cooler.

Serves 4–6

1 flank steak, 2 to 2½ pounds
1 cup dry red wine
¼ cup olive oil
2 tablespoons soy sauce
1 onion, sliced
1 carrot, sliced
2 garlic cloves, smashed
1 teaspoon thyme leaves
½ teaspoon oregano
1 bay leaf
Freshly ground pepper
Salt

1. Trim all excess fat from the meat.

2. In a large bowl or shallow nonaluminum pan, combine the wine, olive oil, soy sauce, onion, carrot, garlic, thyme, oregano and bay leaf to make a marinade.

3. Heavily pepper the beef on both sides and add it to the marinade. Marinate, turning occasionally, for 1½ to 2 hours at room temperature, or longer in the refrigerator or cooler.

4. Remove the meat from the marinade and pat it dry with paper towels; discard the marinade. Salt and pepper the steak heavily on both sides.

5. Grill over a hot fire, or broil about 4 inches from the heat, turning once, for 3 to 4 minutes on each side, or until rare. Let rest, loosely tented with foil to keep warm, for 5 minutes before slicing thinly across the grain on a slight diagonal.

GRILLED EGGPLANT AND ZUCCHINI SLICES

Serves 6–8

1 large firm, shiny eggplant
2 medium zucchini
½ cup olive oil
1 large garlic clove, crushed through a press
1 tablespoon minced fresh basil, or ¼ tea-
    spoon dried
¼ teaspoon salt
⅛ teaspoon freshly ground pepper

1. Cut off the green top of the eggplant, but do not peel. Trim the ends off the zucchini. Cut the vegetables lengthwise into ¼-inch-thick slices.

2. In a small bowl or jar, combine the oil, garlic, basil, salt and pepper.

3. Brush one side of the eggplant and zucchini slices lightly with the seasoned oil, and grill or broil until browned, 3 to 5 minutes. Turn, brush the second side with oil and grill until nicely browned outside and tender inside, 3 to 5 minutes longer.

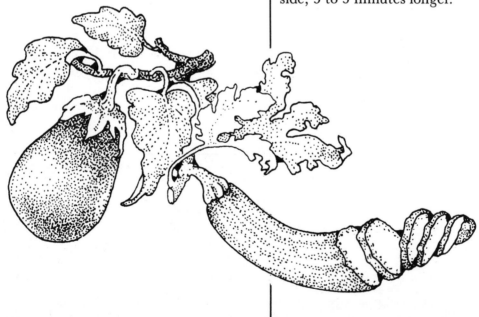

CAULIFLOWER SALAD WITH SUN-DRIED TOMATOES

Sun-dried tomatoes, or *pumate* as they are called in Italian, are one of the latest gourmet favorites. Their intense, dark flavor provides a marvelous foil to the blandness of the cauliflower. Be sure to save the oil for other use when you drain the tomatoes. This pretty salad has all the colors of the Italian flag.

Serves 6–8

1 large cauliflower (1½ to 2 pounds), divided into 1-inch florets
2 tablespoons white wine vinegar
1 teaspoon Dijon-style mustard
¼ teaspoon salt
⅛ teaspoon freshly ground black pepper
⅓ cup olive oil
2 ounces sun-dried tomatoes in olive oil (about 4 halves), drained and cut crosswise into ¼-inch strips
⅓ cup sliced scallion greens

1. In a large saucepan of boiling salted water, blanch the cauliflower until tender but still slightly firm, 5 to 7 minutes; drain.

2. In a medium-size bowl, whisk together the vinegar, mustard, salt and pepper until blended. Gradually whisk in the oil to make a dressing.

3. Add the warm cauliflower and toss to coat. Let stand, tossing occasionally, until cooled to room temperature.

4. Add the tomatoes and scallions and toss lightly. Serve at room temperature or slightly chilled.

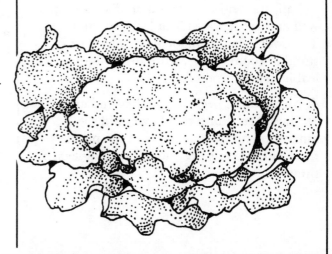

PEACH TURNOVERS

Makes 6

2 cups all-purpose flour
2 tablespoons sugar
½ teaspoon salt
1 stick (4 ounces) unsalted butter
3 tablespoons solid white vegetable
    shortening
2 eggs
3 ripe peaches
1 tablespoon amaretto liqueur
2 tablespoons seedless red raspberry jam

1. In a large bowl, combine the flour, sugar and salt. Cut in the butter and shortening until the mixture resembles coarse meal. Beat one of the eggs lightly and add to the flour mixture. Gather the dough into a ball. If some of the flour doesn't adhere, sprinkle on a few drops of cold water. Divide the dough in half, flatten into two 6-inch disks, wrap well and refrigerate for at least 30 minutes. The dough can be made a day ahead. Let it stand at room temperature until slightly malleable before proceeding.

2. Meanwhile, peel the peaches and cut into ⅜-inch dice. Put into a bowl, add the amaretto and toss to coat. Let the peaches macerate, tossing occasionally, for at least 30 minutes.

3. To assemble the turnovers, preheat the oven to 400°F. On a lightly floured surface, roll out one of the pastry disks a scant ¼ inch thick. With a circular pastry cutter or a pot lid, cut out 3 circles 5 inches in diameter. Leaving a ½-inch border all around, paint each circle with ½ teaspoon raspberry jam. Cover half of each jam circle with about 3 tablespoons, or one-sixth, of the peaches. Moisten the unpainted rims with water, fold over and press the edges of the pastry together. Crimp with a fork to seal. Repeat with the remaining pastry, jam and peaches to make 3 more turnovers.

4. Arrange the turnovers on a heavy cookie sheet. Beat the remaining egg with ½ tablespoon water to make an egg glaze. Brush the tops of the turnovers with the egg glaze.

5. Bake the turnovers in the middle of the oven for about 20 minutes, until the pastry is a light golden brown. Transfer to a rack and let cool. Store at room temperature.

Pool Party

Menu

Serves 6

Cold Shrimp, Served with Creamy Herb Dip (see page 37)

Melon Cubes Wrapped in Prosciutto

Beef, Chicken and/or Chicken Liver Satés with Peanut Dipping Sauce*

Indonesian Pickled Vegetable Salad*

Shrimp Chips or Krupuk

Fresh Pineapple and Strawberries in Kirsch

Chocolate-Frosted Cookies

Special Equipment

Portable grill

Charcoal and matches

Asbestos mitts

Bowl with ice for shrimp

Platters for melon and satés

Toothpicks for melon and shrimp

Bamboo skewers for satés

Small covered container and serving dish for dip

Several small bowls as well as covered container for sauce

Tightly lidded containers or serving dishes for vegetable salad and fruit

Basket for chips

Salad servers and serving spoon

Plate for cookies

Plenty of napkins

Thermos if necessary

Cooler for carrying shrimp, satés and creamy dip

Summer weather and active water sports dictate light food, piquant enough to stimulate dulled appetites, no matter how high the humidity. To my taste, the hot spicy sauces and savory seasonings of Indonesian food are just the thing. It is a marvelous cuisine for entertaining and picnicking because so much of it is prepared ahead of time, and most of it is designed to be served at room temperature.

Assorted satés—Indonesian kebabs—freshly grilled over charcoal and dipped into a spicy-sweet peanut butter sauce, are guaranteed to be the hit of any party. Remember to soak the bamboo skewers in water for at least 1 hour, so they don't burn during grilling. A tart, brightly colored pickled salad is the perfect accompaniment to the satés. Put out baskets of crunchy Chinese shrimp chips, available at Oriental groceries, or if you are up to the work, fry your own *krupuk,* Indonesian chips flavored with shrimp. Copeland Marks, author of *The In-donesian Kitchen,* taught me everything I know about Indonesian cooking, and my recipes are adapted from his.

For starters, be eclectic. I'd choose a couple of light hors d'oeuvres, like cold shrimp and prosciutto and melon cubes, both served with toothpicks or tiny cocktail forks. Refreshing chilled pineapple and ripe strawberries, macerated in kirsch (cherry brandy) for several hours, with a plate of good store-bought cookies makes an easy summer dessert.

BEEF SATES WITH PEANUT DIPPING SAUCE

For these satés you will need thin metal skewers or, more authentically, long bamboo sticks. Be sure to soak wooden skewers in water for at least 1 hour before you use them on the hot grill.

Serves 6–8

2 pounds sirloin steak, cut 1 inch thick and trimmed of excess fat
¼ cup soy sauce
2 tablespoons corn or peanut oil
2 tablespoons water
1 tablespoon molasses
2 garlic cloves, smashed
2 slices of fresh gingerroot (optional)
Peanut Dipping Sauce (recipe follows)

1. Cut the steak into 1-inch cubes.

2. In a medium-size bowl, combine the soy sauce, oil, water, molasses, garlic and gingerroot. Add the beef and marinate at room temperature, tossing occasionally, for at least 30 minutes. For a picnic, throw the meat in with the marinade just before you leave the house; carry it in a cooler.

3. Thread the steak onto skewers, allowing a little space between the cubes. Grill over a hot fire, or broil about 4 inches from the heat, turning, until browned outside and rare or medium-rare, as you prefer, inside, roughly 4 to 6 minutes. Serve hot or at room temperature with Peanut Dipping Sauce.

Chicken Satés Use 2 pounds of skinless, boneless chicken breast or thigh, cut into 1-inch pieces.

Chicken-Liver Satés Chicken livers are cheap, and they make marvelous satés. Use 1½ to 2 pounds. Pat the livers dry. Trim off any green or yellow spots and remove tough connective tubes. Divide the livers into halves and cut each lobe in half if they are large.

PEANUT DIPPING SAUCE

This sauce can be made a day or two ahead and refrigerated, covered. If it thickens upon standing, thin to desired consistency with a little hot water.

Makes about 1 ¼ cups

½ cup hot water
⅔ cup chunky peanut butter
3 tablespoons fresh lemon juice
2 tablespoons soy sauce
2 teaspoons molasses
1 teaspoon sugar

½ teaspoon ground coriander
¼ teaspoon cayenne pepper, or more to taste
2 garlic cloves, crushed through a press
1½ teaspoons minced fresh gingerroot
  (optional)

1. In a small bowl, gradually stir the hot water into the peanut butter until blended.

2. Add the lemon juice, soy sauce, molasses, sugar, coriander, cayenne, garlic and gingerroot. Mix well.

INDONESIAN PICKLED VEGETABLE SALAD

This brightly colored salad is surprisingly good with most grilled or roasted meats. It keeps well in the refrigerator for several days.

Serves 6–8

2 tablespoons peanut or corn oil
1 large garlic clove, minced
1 teaspoon minced fresh gingerroot, or ⅛
     teaspoon powdered ginger
⅓ cup water
2 tablespoons cider vinegar
1 tablespoon sugar
½ teaspoon salt
⅛ teaspoon turmeric
1 medium cucumber, peeled, seeded and cut
     into 1½-by-½-inch sticks
1 small red bell pepper, cut into 1½-by-¼-
     inch julienne strips
1 medium zucchini, cut into 1½-by-½-by-
     ¼-inch sticks
¼ pound green beans, trimmed and cut into
     1- to 1½-inch lengths.

1. In a wok or large skillet, heat the oil over moderate heat. Add the garlic and gingerroot and cook for 10 seconds, until fragrant but not browned.

2. Add the water, vinegar, sugar, salt and turmeric. Bring to a boil, stirring to dissolve the salt and sugar.

3. Add the vegetables, and cook, stirring frequently, for 3 to 5 minutes, until the vegetables are crisp-tender.

4. Pour the vegetables and cooking liquid into a bowl; let cool slightly. Cover and refrigerate for at least 2 hours, or overnight, before serving.

COOKING FOR A CROWD

Concert in the Park

Menu

Serves 10

Sesame-Cheese Biscuits (see page 51)

Young Radishes with Sweet Butter and Thinly Sliced Black Bread

Cold Fillet of Beef with Horseradish Sauce*

Salade Russe*

Asparagus or Heart of Palm Vinaigrette

French Bread (sliced at home)

Assorted Cheeses

Coffee

Cognac

Chocolate Truffles

Special Equipment

Picnic cloth for ground

Basket for biscuits and bread

Butter knife

Covered containers for Horseradish Sauce and Salade Russe

Serving dishes and utensils

Thermos for coffee

Cooler for meat, butter, Salade Russe, cheese (if it is a hot day) and truffles

Cups for coffee and Cognac

It is not uncommon at lawn concerts these days to see people pull out all the stops. From romantic rush baskets lined with calico cloths come feasts fit for a catered affair—fine wines, flowers, even a candelabra or two. At the Glyndebourne Opera outdoor concert in the south of England, it is an annual tradition to picnic in formal dress, with fine bone china, lace tablecloths, lead crystal and sometimes even the butler.

Whatever you are serving on, here is a menu elegant enough to set the occasion, yet simple to serve in appropriate tailgate fashion, assuming you've left your butler at home. Begin with a savory snack of cheese-flavored Sesame-Cheese Biscuits and young radishes, eaten European-style, green leaf and all, with black bread, sweet butter and a pinch of coarse salt.

For the main course there is the buttery tender Cold Fillet of Beef, easy to serve if sliced at home. Carry the Horseradish Sauce separately in a cooler, also packed with the colorful Salade Russe, made of diced potatoes, carrots, beets and peas. Instead of a green salad, which I find bulky for picnics, add a touch of luxury with fresh asparagus or canned hearts of palm vinaigrette.

Bring along an assortment of perfectly ripened cheeses to enjoy with the last of the wine. I like the variety of a Brie, Roquefort, Saint-André and a good chèvre. After such a rich meal, a cup of good strong coffee and a snifter of Cognac is all that's needed, but just to play it safe, I always pack some chocolate truffles for people like me who need at least a touch of sweetness at the end of dinner.

COLD FILLET OF BEEF

Fillet is best when cooked very rare. Remember that the meat will continue to cook upon standing.

Serves 8–12

1 fillet of beef (4 to 5 pounds), trimmed and
    tied
3 tablespoons Cognac
1 tablespoon chopped shallot
3 tablespoons olive oil
Salt and freshly ground pepper

1. Marinate the fillet in the Cognac with the shallot at room temperature, turning occasionally, for 30 to 60 minutes.

2. Preheat the oven to 450°F. Remove the meat from the marinade and pat it dry with paper towels.

3. In a roasting pan or heatproof casserole just large enough to hold the fillet, heat the oil. Add the meat and cook over moderately high heat, turning, until lightly browned all over, about 5 minutes. Season liberally with salt and pepper.

4. Place in the oven and roast uncovered for 20 minutes, or until rare, 135° to 137°F. Transfer the fillet to a rack and let it cool to room temperature; then wrap well and refrigerate. Cut the fillet into ½-inch slices to serve.

HORSERADISH SAUCE

Makes about 2 cups

1 ½ cups sour cream
⅓ cup prepared white horseradish, rinsed
    and drained
½ teaspoon sugar
½ teaspoon salt
4 to 6 tablespoons heavy cream

1. In a small bowl, combine the sour cream, horseradish, sugar and salt; blend well.

2. Gradually stir in the heavy cream by tablespoons until the sauce is the desired consistency, thinned slightly but not runny. (The amount needed will vary, depending upon the thickness of the sour cream.)

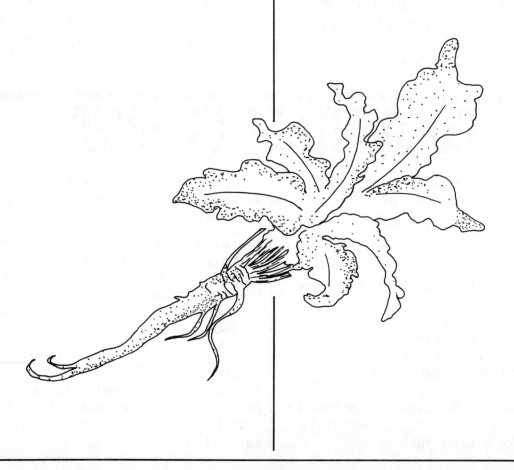

SALADE RUSSE

Serves 8–10

1 bunch of beets (about 1 pound)
3 medium red potatoes (about 1 pound)
¼ cup red wine vinegar
2 tablespoons olive oil
3 medium carrots (about ½ pound), peeled
    and cut into ¼-inch dice
1¼ cups thawed frozen or cooked fresh peas
¾ teaspoon salt
½ teaspoon freshly ground pepper
½ cup mayonnaise

1. Preheat the oven to 375°F. Trim the stems off the beets, leaving 2 inches attached. Wrap the beets in aluminum foil and bake for 1 to 1½ hours, until tender. Let cool for about 15 minutes; then trim off the ends, remove the skin and cut the beets into ¼-inch dice.

2. Meanwhile, cook the potatoes in a saucepan of boiling salted water for 25 to 35 minutes, until tender. Drain and let the potatoes cool for 10 to 15 minutes; then peel and cut them into ¼-inch dice.

3. In another pan of boiling water, cook the diced carrots until just tender, 3 to 4 minutes. Drain well.

4. In a large bowl, toss the warm carrots and potatoes with the vinegar and oil. Let stand, tossing occasionally, for at least 15 minutes.

5. Add the beets and peas to the vegetables; toss to mix. Season with the salt and pepper. Add the mayonnaise and fold until the vegetables are evenly coated and the salad binds together. Place in a bowl, cover and refrigerate until serving time.

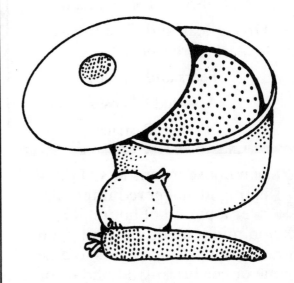

Open House

Menu

Serves 10–20

Tapenade-Stuffed Eggs*

Thinly Sliced Ham and Gruyère Cheese

Country-Style or Duck Pâté

Crusty French Bread

Selection of Mustards

Cherry Tomatoes, Assorted Olives and Cornichons

French-Style Potato Salad*

Green Bean and Shrimp Salad Provençale*

Pears and Apples

Assorted Cheeses

French Pastries

Special Equipment

Covered containers for eggs, potato salad and bean and shrimp salad

Large cooler to carry eggs, potato salad, bean and shrimp salad, ham, cheese and pâté

Platters and serving dishes

Serving utensils

Knives and spreaders for mustard and cheese

Thermos for appropriate beverage

Open house means lots of guests eating at staggered intervals over a period of hours. The occasion might be literally an open house, welcoming friends to a new home or celebrating a holiday, or in true tailgate fashion, you might be sharing your picnic spread with a multitude of neighboring cars. Food should be ample and attractively laid out, in a way that makes replenishing the dishes easy. For an abundant spread like this, I like to combine some of my own entertaining recipes with good-quality simple prepared foods, like cold cuts and pâtés, cheeses and pastry.

For a large informal gathering, whether indoors or out, I put all the food on the table at once, with a coffee urn and dessert off to the side, and let guests help themselves as they wish. Tapenade-Stuffed Eggs, temptingly piquant with bits of black olive, capers, anchovies and garlic, are fabulous for a buffet or picnic.

Arrange attractive platters of sliced ham, Gruyère cheese and good pâté, with crusty French bread to be eaten on the side or sliced into sandwiches. A selection of different mustards and bowls of cherry tomatoes, black and green olives and cornichons, French gherkin pickles, will complement the charcuterie nicely. French-Style Potato Salad, which holds up well at room temperature since it contains no mayonnaise, and a pretty pink and green Bean and Shrimp Salad Provençale make satisfying side dishes.

When choosing the assortment of French pastries for dessert, avoid whipped cream and custard fillings if you expect the pastries to sit out in the sun for any length of time.

TAPENADE-STUFFED EGGS

20 halves

10 hard-cooked eggs
½ cup Mediterranean olives (the black, wrinkled kind), about 2 dozen, rinsed and pitted
1 ounce flat anchovy fillets (half of a 2-ounce tin), rinsed and patted dry
1 tablespoon capers
1 garlic clove, crushed through a press
¼ cup olive oil, preferably extra-virgin
2 teaspoons white wine vinegar
¼ teaspoon freshly ground black pepper
2 dashes of cayenne pepper, or to taste
Tiny capers, for garnish

1. Halve the eggs. I like to cut these crosswise with a v-shaped knife to make decorative little cups. Remove the yolks; set aside ½ yolk separately as garnish. Trim a tiny slice off the bottom of the whites, if necessary, so they stand upright without rocking.

2. In a food processor or blender, combine the olives, anchovies, capers and garlic. Process until chopped. Add the egg yolks, olive oil, vinegar, black pepper and cayenne. Process this tapenade mixture to a coarse paste.

3. Spoon or pipe the tapenade into the egg white halves, mounding it in the center to use all the filling. Sieve the reserved egg yolk half. Garnish each egg with a pinch of sieved egg yolk and a tiny caper, if desired.

FRENCH-STYLE POTATO SALAD

Serves 8–12

3 pounds medium red potatoes
⅓ cup dry white wine
3 tablespoons red wine vinegar
1½ tablespoons Dijon-style mustard
¾ teaspoon salt
½ teaspoon freshly ground pepper
½ cup olive oil
3 medium shallots
Chopped parsley, for garnish

1. Boil the potatoes in a large pot of boiling salted water until just tender, about 25 minutes; drain.

2. As soon as the potatoes are cool enough to handle, peel them and cut into thin slices. In a medium-size bowl, toss the warm potatoes with the wine.

3. In a small bowl, whisk the vinegar, mustard, salt and pepper until blended. Gradually whisk in the oil to make a thick vinaigrette.

4. Pour the dressing over the potatoes, add the shallots, and toss well. Garnish with parsley, if desired.

GREEN BEAN AND SHRIMP SALAD PROVENÇALE

Serves 8–10

1½ pounds green beans
1 pound medium shrimp
2 garlic cloves, crushed through a press
1 teaspoon Dijon-style mustard
½ teaspoon anchovy paste
½ teaspoon *herbes de Provence,* or basil
½ teaspoon salt
¼ teaspoon freshly ground pepper
1 tablespoon fresh lemon juice
2 tablespoons red wine vinegar
⅓ cup olive oil, preferably extra-virgin
½ large sweet onion, thinly sliced

1. In a large pot of boiling salted water, cook the green beans until crisp-tender, about 5 minutes. Drain and rinse under cold running water; drain well.

2. Meanwhile, bring another large saucepan of water to a boil. Add the shrimp and cook until pink and just curled, about 1 minute. Drain. Shell and devein the shrimp.

3. In a small bowl, combine the garlic, mustard, anchovy paste, *herbes de Provence,* salt, pepper, lemon juice, vinegar and olive oil. Whisk to blend well.

4. In a large bowl, toss the green beans and onion lightly to mix. Add the dressing and toss to coat well. Add the shrimp and toss again. Serve at room temperature or slightly chilled.

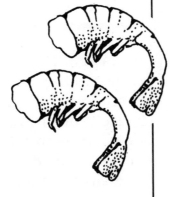

Tennis Party

Menu

Serves 12

Crudités and Whole Boiled Artichokes with Gorgonzola Dip*

Melon Cubes Wrapped in Prosciutto

Thinly Sliced Speck and Hard Salami

Caponata*

Tuna and White-Bean Salad*

Lemon and Lime Seafood Salad (see page 53)

Gorgonzola Dolcelatte, Taleggio and Parmesan Cheese

White and Whole-Wheat Italian Bread (sliced at home)

Black Grapes, Pears and Whole Strawberries

Assorted Italian Pastries

Espresso with Anisette

Special Equipment

Basket for *crudités* and bowl for dip

Toothpicks for melon

Cocktail napkins

Covered containers for transporting dip, tuna and bean salad, Caponata and seafood salad

Serving dishes and utensils

Cheeseboard and knives

Basket for bread

Bowl for fruits

Platter for pastries

Thermos for espresso

Large cooler for carrying dip, salads and cheese (if it is a hot day)

This is a fabulous spread for a large crowd, and it's modeled after a tennis party I prepared years ago. Like many young cooks trying to break into the food business, I used to cater parties in my spare time on weekends. My favorite client—both because she was my best customer and because she appreciated the food and the extra touches I put into it so much—was

Ruth Norek, for whom I created this menu. It was a buffet party for 50 at an indoor tennis court, but it could be served outdoors in summer as well. In true tailgate fashion everything had to be transported; there were no food preparation facilities and no refrigeration. The food had to sit out for at least 3 hours. This menu, with an assortment of marinated salads, which taste better after standing for a bit, worked beautifully. The recipes, as indicated, serve 12, but they can be doubled easily.

To capture the theme of the tennis party, I asked an Italian baker to make giant loaves of bread shaped like tennis rackets and rolls formed into tennis balls. It was a huge success. If you try, you may be able to find an accommodating baker to carry out the theme of your tailgate party.

For this easy-to-serve buffet, everyone can help themselves, and only forks and large serving spoons are needed. You can serve the *crudités* and dip, melon with prosciutto and *speck* first as appetizers, or put out the entire spread at once. Speck is cured pork shoulder, similar to prosciutto, but more flavorful because it is lightly smoked. If you cannot find it in an Italian grocery or specialty food shop in your area, substitute prosciutto, a good Genoa salami or assorted Italian cold cuts. Large boiled artichokes are deliciously attractive additions to the usual complement of raw vegetables.

Tip for setting out the fruit: If you have a grapevine or any wild ones growing near you, pick a bunch of large leaves. Use them to line shallow baskets in which to arrange the fruits. Add peaches or nectarines too if you have them. The dark green leaves make a beautiful foil for the bright fruits, a simple but spectacular presentation.

I like to offer cheese at the end of the meal, to avoid filling up on it, and because the flavor is more appreciated when it is enjoyed as a separate course. If you prefer, however, you can put it out with the appetizers. Serve lots of good Chianti, such as Antinori or Ruffino.

Afterwards, let everyone help themselves to fruits and pastries, if they still have room. Pour small cups of espresso. Bring a bottle of anisette with you, or add some of the liqueur to the coffee thermos just before you leave.

GORGONZOLA DIP

Double the recipe to serve 12.

Makes about 1 ⅓ cups

4 ounces Gorgonzola cheese, at room
    temperature
½ cup sour cream
¼ cup mayonnaise
¼ to ⅓ cup heavy cream
1 tablespoon Cognac
Dash of cayenne pepper

1. In a small bowl or in a food processor, mash the Gorgonzola cheese. Gradually mix in the sour cream and mayonnaise until blended. Stir in ¼ cup of the heavy cream, the Cognac and cayenne.

2. If the dip is too thick, or if it thickens upon standing, thin out with a little more heavy cream. Cover and refrigerate until serving time.

CAPONATA

Traditionally, this dish is made with anchovies, but I leave them out because so many people dislike them, and I don't think it needs them. Untraditionally, I roast the eggplant and pepper for a mellow, slightly smoky flavor. As with many highly seasoned tomatoey dishes, this improves overnight in the refrigerator. Caponata can be served as a vegetable or a salad or as a spread for an hors d'oeuvre. It can be served chilled or at room temperature, which I prefer.

Serves 8 to 12

1 large eggplant
1 large green bell pepper
⅓ cup olive oil, preferably extra-virgin
2 large onions, cut into ½-inch squares
3 celery ribs with leafy tops, cut into ¼-inch
    dice
2 large garlic cloves, minced
1 can (28 ounces) Italian-style peeled toma-
    toes, seeded, drained and coarsely
    chopped
2 tablespoons tomato paste
¼ cup chopped brine-cured olives, prefera-
    bly green
2 ½ tablespoons capers, chopped if large

2 tablespoons red wine vinegar
2 teaspoons sugar
2 teaspoons salt
¾ teaspoon oregano
⅛ teaspoon crushed hot red pepper
1 tablespoon chopped flat-leaf parsley
¼ teaspoon freshly ground black pepper, or
    more to taste

1. Punch a few holes in the eggplant with a fork or knife. If you have a gas stove, cook the eggplant and pepper directly on the flame, turning until charred all over. If not, broil the vegetables as close to the heat as possible to achieve the same results. The eggplant will soften, but don't let it get completely mushy.

2. Remove the top from the eggplant. Peel off the skin. If it doesn't come off easily, scrape the flesh from the skin with a knife. Rub the charred skin off the pepper. Stem and seed the pepper. Cut the vegetables roughly into ½-inch dice.

3. Heat the oil in a large nonaluminum flameproof casserole. Add the onions and sauté over moderately high heat until they begin to brown, 3 to 5 minutes.

4. Add the celery, reduce the heat to moderate and cook until softened, about 5 minutes longer. Add half the garlic and cook for 1 minute.

5. Add the eggplant, pepper, tomatoes, tomato paste, olives, capers, vinegar, sugar, salt, oregano and hot pepper. Cook, partially covered, for about 20 minutes, or until most of the liquid is evaporated.

6. Stir in the parsley, black pepper and remaining garlic.

TUNA AND WHITE BEAN SALAD

This party salad keeps well, covered, in the refrigerator for up to 3 days.

Serves 8–12

1 pound dried white beans (I prefer white
    pea beans, but you can use Great North-
    ern white or cannellini beans)
¼ cup olive oil, preferably extra-virgin
¼ cup red wine vinegar
2 tablespoons fresh lemon juice
1 large garlic clove, crushed through a press
2 teaspoons salt
¼ teaspoon freshly ground pepper
1 can (7 ounces) Italian tuna in olive oil,
    drained and flaked
⅔ cup thinly sliced scallions (3 to 4)
⅓ cup chopped parsley

1. Rinse the beans and pick them over to remove any grit. Place in a large pot and add enough water to cover by 2 inches. Bring to a boil, remove from the heat and let stand, covered, for 1 hour; or soak in cold water overnight.

2. Drain the beans. Return them to the pot and add fresh water to cover by at least 2 inches; do not add any salt. Bring to a boil, reduce the heat, and simmer until the beans are tender and creamy but still retain a little

resistance to the bite, 45 minutes to 1 ½ hours, depending on the beans. Drain and transfer to a large bowl.

3. While the beans are still warm, add the oil, vinegar, lemon juice, garlic, salt and pepper. Toss well to mix. Let stand, tossing occasionally, until cooled to room temperature, about 1 hour.

4. Add the tuna, scallions and parsley and toss to mix. Serve at room temperature or slightly chilled.

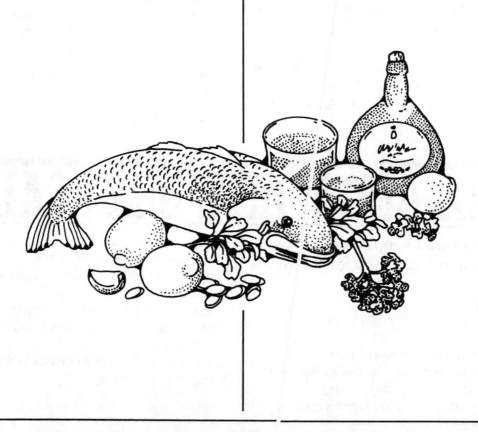

Labor Day

Menu

Serves 12–18

Barbecued Spareribs*

Barbecued Chicken (see page 81)

Potato Salad

Coleslaw

Sliced Tomatoes and Cucumbers

Buttermilk Cornbread Squares*

Cold Beer

Chocolate Fudge Cake*

Special Equipment

Large covered containers for carrying ribs and chicken

Covered containers for potato salad and coleslaw

Domed cake platter for packing cake

Ice chest for beer

Large cooler or second ice chest to carry chicken, ribs, potato salad and coleslaw

Portable grill, preferably 2

Charcoal and matches

Asbestos mitts

2 long-handled forks

Platters and serving forks for ribs, chicken and sliced tomatoes and cucumbers

Bowls and serving spoons for potato salad and coleslaw

Basket for cornbread squares

Cake knife

The last official holiday before school begins often serves as an occasion for that nostalgic final barbecue of summer. Here is a spread big enough for all the family and friends you want to invite.

Barbecued chicken and ribs are traditional favorites, with good reason. Bring plenty of both, because if your guests are anything like mine, they'll all want some of each and come back for seconds and thirds. The chicken marinates in its sauce during the day, and the ribs are pre-baked to minimize grilling time and insure tender, well-cooked meat.

Serve heaps of potato salad and coleslaw—your own (see recipes on pages 82 and 62) or store-bought—and a large platter of sliced fresh tomatoes and cucumbers. Buttermilk Cornbread Squares are an added treat. Wrap them in aluminum foil and warm on the edge of the grill just before serving with lots of sweet butter. Have plenty of cold lager beer on ice. For dessert, there's an all-American favorite, Chocolate Fudge Cake, this one courtesy of my editor, Harriet Bell.

BARBECUED SPARERIBS

The recipe for these tastiest of ribs was given to me by Charles MacPhee, a distinguished writer I met at the home of Italian cooking teacher Anna Teresa Callen.

Double, triple or quadruple the recipe below to have enough for the expected number of guests.

Serves 4–6

4 pounds pork spareribs, separated
1 cup cider vinegar
⅓ cup ketchup
2 tablespoons Worcestershire sauce
1 to 2 tablespoons liquid smoke, preferably
    Wright's (optional)
1 tablespoon sugar
1 teaspoon dry mustard
1 teaspoon ground cumin
1 teaspoon salt
½ teaspoon paprika
1 small onion, minced
2 garlic cloves, minced
Dash of Tabasco, or more to taste (I use at
    least ¼ teaspoon)

1. Preheat the oven to 350°F. Roast the ribs on a rack in a roasting pan for 1 hour.

2. Meanwhile, in a small nonaluminum saucepan, combine the remaining ingredients to make the barbecue sauce. Bring to a boil, reduce the heat slightly and simmer for about 15 minutes to reduce and thicken the sauce slightly. Remove from the heat and let cool.

3. If you are finishing the ribs on a grill at your tailgate, remove them from the oven at this point. Brush all over with the barbecue sauce. Let them cool, then wrap well and refrigerate. Cover the sauce and refrigerate it separately. This can be done a day ahead.

4. To finish the ribs in the oven, baste them after 1 hour and continue cooking, basting every 5 to 10 minutes, for about 30 minutes, until the ribs are fully cooked.

5. To finish the ribs on a grill, light the coals about 45 minutes before you plan to eat. Grill the ribs 4 to 6 inches from the heat, basting every 5 minutes, until completely cooked and tender but not scorched, 15 to 20 minutes.

BUTTERMILK CORNBREAD SQUARES

Makes 18 squares

2 cups yellow cornmeal
1 cup all-purpose flour
3 tablespoons sugar
1 tablespoon baking powder
½ teaspoon baking soda
1 teaspoon salt
2 eggs, lightly beaten
2 cups buttermilk
6 tablespoons unsalted butter, melted and
    cooled slightly

1. Preheat the oven to 425°F. Grease a baking dish 13 by 8 inches. Place in the oven to heat.

2. Sift together the cornmeal, flour, sugar, baking powder, baking soda and salt into a large bowl.

3. Add the eggs, buttermilk and melted butter. Stir until just barely blended; there should still be small lumps and pockets of dry ingredients (do not overmix).

4. Pour the batter into the hot baking dish and bake for 25 minutes, or until the cornbread is golden brown on top and a tester inserted in the center comes out clean.

CHOCOLATE FUDGE CAKE

1 stick (4 ounces) unsalted butter
3 eggs, separated, yolks lightly beaten
2½ cups sugar
2½ cups cake flour
1½ cups milk
3 squares (3 ounces) unsweetened chocolate,
    melted
2 teaspoons baking powder
2 teaspoons vanilla

Chocolate Satin Icing

1 cup sugar
¼ cup cornstarch
¼ teaspoon salt
1 cup boiling water
2 squares (2 ounces) unsweetened chocolate,
    melted
3 tablespoons unsalted butter

1. Preheat the oven to 325°F. Butter and flour two 8-inch round cake pans.

2. In the large bowl of an electric mixer, cream the butter well. Add the egg yolks and beat the mixture well.

3. Slowly add the sugar. Alternately mix in the flour and milk. Mix in the melted chocolate.

4. In a separate bowl, beat the egg whites until they are stiff but not dry. Add the baking powder and vanilla to the egg whites.

5. Fold the egg whites into the chocolate batter, blending well until no white streaks show.

6. Pour the batter into the prepared cake pans and bake for 40 minutes, or until a tester inserted into the center of the cake comes out clean.

7. Remove the cake pans from the oven and let them cool on a wire rack for 15 to 20 minutes. Gently unmold the layers from the pans and let them cool completely on the rack.

8. To prepare the icing, combine the sugar, cornstarch and salt in a saucepan. Add the boiling water and cook, stirring constantly over low heat, until the icing is smooth and thick. Add the melted chocolate and butter and blend until smooth. Let the icing cool to room temperature.

9. Cover one of the cake layers with about one-third of the icing. Top with the second layer and frost the top and sides of the cake generously with the remaining icing.

Source Guide

The Chef's Catalog
3915 Commercial Avenue
Northbrook, IL 60062
(312) 480-9400

Cooktique
9 Railroad Avenue
Tenafly, NJ 07670
(201) 568-7990

Hammacher Schlemmer
147 East 57th Street
New York, NY 10022
(212) 421-9000

The Horchow Collection
P.O. Box 340257
Dallas, TX 75234
(800) 527-0303;
In Texas, (800) 442-5806;
   in Dallas (800) 980-4040

L. L. Bean
Freeport, ME 04033
(207) 865-3111

Spiegel Catalog
P.O. Box 7623
Chicago, IL 60680
(800) 345-4500

Thermos
Customer Service Dept.
Thermos Avenue
Norwich, CT 06360
(800) 243-0745

Tupperware Home Parties
Consult your local white pages or contact:
Customer Service Dept.
P.O. Box 2353
Orlando, FL 32802
(305) 847-3111

Weber "Go-Anywhere" Grills
Weber-Stephen Products Co.
200 East Daniels Road
Palatine, IL 60067
(312) 934-5800

Williams-Sonoma
Mail Order Dept.
P.O. Box 7456
San Francisco, CA 94120-7456
(415) 652-9007

Index